BILL ADLER'S
CHANCE OF A LIFETIME

BILL ADLER'S

CHANCE OF A LIFETIME

WARNER BOOKS

A Warner Communications Company

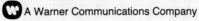 A Warner Communications Company

Printed in the United States of America
First Printing: August 1985
10 9 8 7 6 5 4 3 2 1

Library of Congress Cataloging in Publication Data

Adler, Bill.
    Bill Adler's Chance of a lifetime.

    1. New business enterprises.   2. Small business.
I. Title.   II. Title: Chance of a lifetime.
HD62.5.A35   1985   658'.022   85-40008
ISBN 0-446-51327-X

Designed by Giorgetta Bell McRee

Contents

A PERSONAL MESSAGE FROM BILL ADLER

The introductions to most books are too long and wordy so I am going to keep this simple and to the point.

Within these pages, you will find everything you have to know about starting your own business—whether you have had any previous experience or not.

You will also find inspiring stories about other people just like you who have started their own businesses and who now have financial independence.

I believe that virtually everybody can succeed on their own if they are willing to work hard. Since you have bought this book, I am assuming this means you.

Even if I weren't offering $25,000 to somebody to start their own business, this book would be invaluable for anyone who wants to go into business for himself or herself—whether on a part-time or a full-time basis.

But of course, I am going to give somebody $25,000 to start his or her business and I really hope it will be you.

If you read the instructions on page 211 and read this book, your chances of getting my check for $25,000 are as good as anybody else's. And, that check will definitely be given away to somebody. I don't want the money anymore. I want it in the hands of some deserving person who wants that chance of a lifetime.

I have done my part. I have written the book telling you everything you have to know about going into your own business and I have come up with the $25,000.

Now the rest is up to you. Don't let me down. As a matter of fact, don't let yourself down. This is truly your chance of a lifetime!

Bill Adler

The Second Golden Age of Entrepreneurship

❑ In 1983 Donna Pearson tried to telephone for a pizza delivery during a party at her apartment in Albuquerque, but was unable to find a pizzeria that offered such a service. So she started "Pizza on Call," a business delivering pizza to telephone customers, and now has two helpers working for her. She will net $20,500 in 1984!

❑ In 1981 Donald C. Burr founded People Express Airlines and built it into a multi-million dollar company with over 2,600 workers on its payroll—one of the few recent success stories in the now turbulent airline industry. He did it by parlaying a simple idea—"no frills flying"—into a major enterprise.

❑ In 1982 Jack Hart of Miami wanted to buy a jacket with a painting of a Jack of Hearts on the back, but he couldn't find any ready-made. Using acrylic paint, he created his own design on a denim jacket, and later sold it to an admirer for $50. Now he's in business for himself, with orders three months ahead of his output—and a bank account twice what he had when he worked for a trucking firm.

1

❑ In 1976 computer wizards Steven Jobs and Stephen Wozniak started a personal computer company from scratch, calling it Apple Computer, and within six years built it into a multi-million dollar business employing 4,000 people. They began by selling a Volkswagen microbus and investing the money in nothing more than a simple idea.

❑ In 1980 the Watkins family found their sprawling, 1790 Colonial farmhouse within sight of a relocated main highway into a major Northeastern city. Capitalizing on the potential of their picturesque setting and authentic New England decor, they transformed the house into The Colonial Tavern. Elated by the success of the venture, they now plan to add an antique shop.

As exemplified by the above instances, there is a surge of activity in the business world today, signaling the start of the second golden age of entrepreneurship in America. The first occurred at the end of the nineteenth century, when the country was shifting from an agrarian to an industrialized society.

The heroes of that transformation were the men who founded the great oil, automobile, steel, and chemical empires that still dominate the industrialized world. In those days the entrepreneur was known not for his acumen and gumption but for his "rugged individualism"— which later became a dirty word in political circles.

The first golden age of entrepreneurship gradually ended when the golden age of giant corporations began in the early twentieth century. These huge companies employed the bulk of American workers, blue collar and white collar. Yet in the 1960s and 1970s, something happened to change all that. The trend toward everybody being employed by the big companies slowed down and finally reversed itself.

The Change in Direction

Since the late 1970s, big business—those companies exemplified by the *Fortune* 500—has lost over 1.5 million jobs. At the same time small businesses—those run by entrepreneurs—have provided some 8 or 9 million new jobs between 1977 and 1982. Statistics show that the *Fortune* 500 companies provide less employment than they did in 1969.

There are many reasons for this about-face, but most observers of the economic scene attribute it to another transformation in the nation's economy—the change from what came to be known as the smokestack-industry economy to the developing information-based service company economy.

As our economy becomes dependent on the control and dissemination of information and its attendant services, it must shift its emphasis from general management skills in the handling of large numbers of men and women in a work-force environment to the quick and accurate storage and retrieval of vital information needed for high-tech achievement.

The Entrepreneur's Role Today

It is today's entrepreneur who can develop new products and services to accommodate this demand, generating new jobs, forcing older established companies to become more efficient, and toughening the country's competitiveness against outsiders.

Today's entrepreneur must build organizations radically different from the traditional companies that made America great. The ability to adapt to new pressures will make the country move ahead, not the ability to settle down into the ease and affluence of corporate middle management.

And today's entrepreneur is making his—and her—mark. New business incorporations reached a record 600,000 in 1983. Although the glamour of entrepreneurship is usually associated with the more visible high-tech operators, there are thousands of small businesspersons running shops in the middle of crowded city streets or busily making products in the quiet of their own homes.

Every person who is self-employed—some 8 million today: one million more than two years ago—should consider himself or herself an entrepreneur. To manage any kind of enterprise takes initiative, drive, and imagination, and separates the entrepreneur from the person who is content to work in comfortable docility for someone else.

Shopkeeping, craftsmanship, contractual production, services of all kinds, consultantships, professional advice—all these jobs contribute to the economy and allow the proprietor or professional to work and earn as much as and sometimes more than the typical employee.

The Rise of Small Business

The ratio of people employed in small businesses compared to those in large businesses has been increasing. Between 1976 and 1980, small business accounted for about 35 percent of total private employment. During that period, small businesses were responsible for the generation of 51 percent of all new jobs.

During 1981 and 1982, about one million new businesses were formed, creating a net gain of some one million jobs in the economy, offsetting massive layoffs in the steel, auto, and other basic smokestack industries. Small business was carrying most of the load to ease the economic dislocation caused by the inability of American industry to compete worldwide.

The revolutionary changes in the world economy that stimulated the rise of today's entrepreneur did not occur by magic. The government made it attractive for individuals to get into the act. One of the greatest deterrents to individual proprietorship was the enormously high capital gains tax one had to pay if an enterprise proved successful.

Soaking the Rich

The rationale for this tax was derived from good old American grass-roots populism: soak the rich. To soak the rich, the government in 1969 increased from 25 percent to 49 percent the maximum tax on long-term capital gains—profit made on the sale of stocks and other property. That meant that one half of every dollar earned in profits went to the government!

The effect on the opening of new small businesses—those operated by entrepreneurs—was devastating. Within five years, the number of new ventures had declined by one third. Finally, in 1978, the government, realizing that there were few small businesses starting up, got wise and acted. The taxation rate on capital gains was cut back from 49 percent to 28 percent. And then, in another cutback, the rate was finally reduced to 20 percent in 1981. That was the year the floodgates opened and the individual proprietor—known in this new era as the "entrepreneur"—came into his own again.

Says entrepreneur John Moss, the founder of BPI Systems, a software firm in Austin, Texas:

> There has never been a better time to start a business than right now. The climate is exactly right.

And Frank Swain of the Small Business Administration says:

> This may be a good time to start a business if you know what your costs are going to be.

Something else has happened. The public's attitude about entrepreneurs—who used to be sneered at as "rugged individualists" during the 1960s and 1970s—has changed about 180 degrees.

The Challenge for America

For example, in the "Swinging Sixties" Jerry Rubin was a radical campus upstart—anti-capitalist, anti-business, and generally anti-establishment. Yet he said in a bylined 1980 article in the *New York Times*:

> The challenge for American capitalism in the eighties is to bring the entrepreneurial spirit back to America. The large corporations have discouraged people's expression and ambition. America needs a revitalization of the small business spirit.

The founder of People Express Airlines puts it in an even more positive form:

> Entrepreneurship will be the major impetus of the decade immediately ahead of us—and what's ahead is terrifically exciting.

Karl H. Vesper, professor of entrepreneurship at the University of Washington, says:

> Clearly, there's been a radical rise of entrepreneurship. There's a latent lust for it in all of us— it's the American way.

One small-business entrepreneur sees it from another important angle:

> Perhaps the phenomenon we are witnessing now has less to do with action or risk-taking than with the simple observation that *people,* not institutions, create economic wealth. In this respect, perhaps the entrepreneur is leading all of corpo-

rate America to a rediscovery of business as enterprise, a rediscovery of business as a process limited only by the boundaries of each individual's intelligence, imagination, energy, and daring.

After all, it was the spirit of rugged individualism that built America in the first place and allowed such inventive geniuses as Thomas A. Edison, Cyrus H. McCormick, Isaac M. Singer, Robert Fulton, and dozens of others to build that "better mousetrap" and move the country full-speed ahead into the Industrial Age.

The point is that rugged individualism is not dead; high-tech entrepreneurship has proved that. Yet people today are apt to fall into passivity and surrender, feeling there are no new worlds to conquer, no new inventions to invent, no new enterprises to mount.

That concept is *absolutely false.* However, it is a fact of life that the typical white-collar or blue-collar worker in industry who has any kind of creative talent is pretty much struggling in a job trap that was not conceived to restrict, but has surely proved to do so.

This is perfectly illustrated by an analysis of what happens when the typical worker becomes unemployed.

Does the unemployed worker start a business on his or her own? Usually not. What happens is that such a person becomes a part of the welfare system; once out of a job, the unemployed individual begins to live on insurance money generated by the system itself in conjunction with the government.

The New Continental Way

In England and France, the governments have begun a revolutionary system to help unemployed people open their own businesses. The idea is to let those who are out of work use the money owed to them from the unemployment insurance system to stake themselves to a business.

Although this system was denounced at first by politicians, it has turned out to be a total success. Recent figures show that 63,000 unemployed individuals in England, who would have continued to be out of work if the opportunity had not been open to them to do something on their own, are now running their own shops! In France the figure is 75,000 back to work on their own.

Entrepreneurial Advantage

In America most entrepreneurs get started by discovering a market niche that big companies find too small to fill. The individual who spots that niche does not have to go through the lengthy review procedures that a large corporation must use, and can move quickly from development to finished products unencumbered by corporate bottlenecks.

One venture capital executive explains:

> The small entrepreneur can make decisions fast and can develop commercial technology faster than is possible in a large corporation. So for certain types of projects, a small corporation is the most effective vehicle.

This is the advantage that any individual has in competition with a superpower corporation. The government itself has also begun helping small companies by deregulating airlines, financial services, trucking, and telecommunications industries, thus breaking the large companies' government-protected stranglehold on their industries.

Today's Women Entrepreneurs

A new source of entrepreneurial energy comes from the women in the work force. Although there have been changing attitudes about women in business lately, they have not really changed fast enough to satisfy the many who want to compete on an equal basis with men.

More and more, American women are beating their heads against the "cement ceiling" of the business hierarchy, finding it impossible to rise above a certain level in the corporate environment. As more and more of them bump their heads against this invisible yet very real ceiling, more and more of them will opt for different methods of scaling the heights—methods that do not require advancement up a prescribed set of steps into the upper regions of influence and clout. And money.

And more and more, women are finding that the best place to compete head to head with men—no holds barred, no handicaps allowed, in hand-to-hand combat— is in individual proprietorship, in unadorned, vigorous, and inventive entrepreneurship. For a woman on her own in a business does not have the frustrating one-on-one adversarial conflict she experiences in a company. She can make whatever profits she is able to, with no one above her allocating a larger share of the profit pie to a man doing the same job as she.

There is another reason women find they can make their way more quickly and with less opposition when they work on their own rather than in a group. Not only are they discriminated against because they are women, but they are discriminated against because they lack the "proper" credentials to get the "right"—translation: high-paying—job.

In 1978 the White House appointed a Task Force on Women Business Owners, and this survey found that "the growth rate for self-employed women as a group was three times that of self-employed men from 1972 to 1977."

Statistics from the Small Business Administration, a government agency set up to aid small businesses, shows that between 1980 and 1982, the number of self-employed women increased by 213,000, or 10 percent, to a total of 2.3 million. During the same years, the number of self-employed men increased by only 47,000, or 1 percent, to 5 million.

9

Thus it is clear that today business ownership is a fertile field for dissatisfied, ambitious women.

Words from the Wise

Charlotte Taylor puts it this way in *Women in the Business Game:*

> When you are bright and you feel thwarted, you leave the workplace for the marketplace.

And:

> For many women, ownership is the fastest track to the economic mainstream.

Mary Kay Ash, founder of Mary Kay Cosmetics Inc., has said:

> When you are on your own, you get paid what you are worth, not what your job is worth.

Mary Kay started out on her own after working for a direct-mail company which kept passing her up on the promotion list time after time: .

> The only way a woman can get into a high business level is through being an entrepreneur and going into a business she can control.

Not everyone who has an idea for a product or a service has the good luck to be rich enough to strike out on his or her own immediately. In fact, the vast majority of potential entrepreneurs are without funds. This creates a problem. If no one but the rich can become entrepreneurs—and the rich don't need to make money anyway— what's going to happen to the spirit of entrepreneurship?

The Fountainhead of Seed Money

Luckily, there is seed money available. For example, the seed money provided by the contest run in conjunction with the publication of this book is partly derived from a source of funds for people with good business ideas. The $25,000 offered to the person who can prove himself or herself the most proficient in projecting a new enterprise is enough to get a good business going.

And there are other sources of funds for those without. People with large sums of money at their command know that a successful venture can pay off within a very few years. Even if a venture proves to be unfruitful, there may be a tax advantage for the backer or backers.

Funds allocated to new enterprises are known as "venture capital"—and a company providing such funds is known as a "venture capital business." Typically, such an organization is a partnership or consortium of investors. No one who invests money does it simply for kicks. Even if such a venture can be used as a tax write-off if the money goes down the drain, the venture capitalist is always *hoping* some tangible profit will come out of his or her investment.

And so such seed money is provided to the fledgling entrepreneur in return for an equity stake in the business, usually from 30 percent to 60 percent of the company. Then, ten years later, when the new company goes public or is sold to a bigger corporation, the original investor recoups his or her money, and sometimes a lot more in addition.

The returns range in the 20 percent to 30 percent pretax area, although some returns are over 50 percent. In 1983 a total of 825 companies went public, with a $10.5 billion profit in toto!

No wonder there are more than 1,000 venture capital funds to be tapped by the entrepreneur. In fact, accord-

11

ing to *Venture Capital Journal,* a trade publication serving venture capitalists, more than $4 billion was raised in 1983, expanding the pool of venture capital funds to $11.5 billion in all.

That's a lot of money for entrepreneurs to try to get!

Getting Access to Greater Funds

Says a report to Congress submitted by the Inter-Agency Task Force on Small Business Finance, a study group:

> There is a greater variety of sources and meth-
> ods of small-business financing now than there
> was twenty years ago, suggesting that small busi-
> ness may have greater access to funds now than
> at that time.

The problem is that venture capitalists are a picky lot, much like bankers with their staid ideas of selectivity and conservatism. While the money is there for the taking, the person who does the taking must show extremely attractive business potential to the people charged with the allocation of the money.

Not every entrepreneur is going to find the amount of venture capital that was found at Venrock, the Rockefeller family fund that was tapped to start Apple Computer. These people typically are steely-eyed, tight-lipped, and tough. Only one in thirty-three—about 3 percent—of the entrepreneurs who try to raise money actually get it.

In fact, one observer of the venture capital scene says that for every 1,000 entrepreneurs qualified to get a sizable investment, only one venture capitalist will decide to advance the money.

Teaching the Fundamentals

Today's increasing interest in entrepreneurship is responsible for opening the educational system to the needs of people aiming to start their own businesses. There are almost 160 schools that now offer courses in individual proprietorship; in 1970 there were only sixteen. Even at Harvard, the most traditional of all business schools, two out of three students now take entrepreneurial management courses.

There are more than 200 community colleges throughout the country that offer small-business courses, according to a Small Business Association survey.

One of the most interesting findings surfacing from this investigation is that the individual who has the most success in assimilating the elements of the standard business curriculum—and achieves the highest grades—will most probably fit easily into the corporate structure of a big company.

However, the person who can be molded into the perfect cog for the corporate machine does not always have the potential to become a successful entrepreneur. The psychological elements found in a contentious, adversarial, risk-taking type who will be a good entrepreneur, are not found in the amenable, adaptable, flexible, self-assured type who will be a good corporate cog.

The Value of Money

Many vociferous sixties radicals did not try to accumulate money. In fact, since many of them came from affluent families and could always depend on a check from home if the commune's profits were down for the month, many scorned the acquisition of money, unlike the entrepreneur of today whose chief satisfaction lies in the successful—and rapid—accumulation of money.

Says Mitchell Kapor, the successful entrepreneur who founded the Lotus Development Corporation:

> Money is back in vogue and the people who start businesses and are successful are bearers of the cultural standard. The sixties generation has matured. There's been a generational decision that

society is worth salvaging. It's not that institutions per se are corrupt. But it requires a dedicated effort to create institutions that treat people well, provide value, and are profitable.

A business school professor puts it this way:

Money is the long hair of the eighties.

Clearly, the desire to make money is one of the predominant reasons the entrepreneur wants to go out on his or her own. But the desire for the fulfillment and excitement of running a business is also part and parcel of the psychological profile of the entrepreneur.

Following the Leader

Do not for a moment think that the entrepreneur is an unexceptional person. There are far fewer natural-born entrepreneurs than there are natural-born workers. The ratio is about the same as leaders to followers.

You can often assume that a misfit in an office job is an entrepreneur trying to call attention to himself or herself, but this is not always true. Every misfit does not possess the peculiar qualities that make up the true entrepreneur. In fact, the entrepreneur fits a special pattern of personality and character.

Not everyone can be a successful entrepreneur. Nor should everyone *try* to be an entrepreneur. To try and fail is to waste days, months, and years in a futile quest for the unattainable. You should first of all determine whether you have the physical stamina, the psychological profile, and the character elements that go to make up a successful entrepreneur.

In addition, you must determine whether you have the real *desire* to run a business, to make money, to boss other people around—in short, to be one of the handful of movers and shakers in the business world today.

Then, once you have determined that, you can proceed to draw up a plan in order to attract venture capital to back you in your business ventures.

2

What It Takes to Be an Entrepreneur

A CASE HISTORY: I

Annette grew up thinking she was bright enough, but somehow she never seemed to make good grades throughout her schooling. In spite of the fact that her high school scores were mediocre, she was able to get into college, and once again graduated with a middling-to-average record. The problem was her test scores. She was a whiz in class, but a dud at the bluebook.

Restless and ambitious, she determined after graduation not to settle down and get married immediately. She wanted to try to make her mark in business. She felt she would be very good in an office job.

The first job she got seemed perfect; she was a file clerk for a large law firm. Immediately she sensed that the filing system was inefficient and that the people in charge of it almost as inefficient as the system itself. She set about changing it. After interminable arguments with her superiors, she was finally fired.

Finding the Proper Niche

She took a secretarial course, flunked it, and then got another job, this time with a large corporation. Turning over a new leaf, Annette determined to get along with everyone and settle down into a niche proper for a professional woman office worker.

But she quickly perceived that the office where she worked was not being run effectively. She tried to institute changes, at first by suggesting them mildly, and then by showing that they truly did work. Nevertheless, in spite of the success of several of her ideas, she was looked upon by her superiors as a troublemaker.

Within nine months she was fired once again, this time not only for disobeying a superior but for sassing him with words that were "not quite ladylike."

Annette took to psychoanalysis, but found it was costing her too much money and was producing no tangible results. After six months she quit and decided to get another job. This time she hired on as a bookkeeper. Oddly enough, in spite of her bad grades in school, she was a whiz at finances. At first everything went swimmingly for her, but then she began to question the way the office functioned, particularly in its systems setup.

The Only Way Out: Do It Yourself

After a series of confrontations with her boss, she was fired once again. But now she was finding it difficult even to land a job interview. Her whole background was well known, and her résumé reflected her inability to perform satisfactorily.

She tried selling household aids door to door, but with most women working and not at home she found it was

16

not the time for selling that way. She tried clerking at a department store, but found that intolerably boring and finally was fired after an altercation with a rude customer.

But Annette determined to succeed somehow in business and resolved to open a store of her own.

A CASE HISTORY: II

Martin was the virtual antithesis of Annette. He was inoffensively intelligent, charming, and unassuming. In school he was always the most popular person in class, and he was very good in his schoolwork as well. When the teacher read a model paper out loud, it was usually Martin's. He was complimented on his diction, on his vocabulary, and on his ability to communicate.

He continued his amazing progress in college, and after graduation went off to business school. He chose one of the best business schools in the country, and while there distinguished himself with his papers and his ability to demonstrate how to run a business.

In addition, he was editor of the college's magazine, famed for its excellence. When he graduated, he was scouted by a half dozen huge corporations, and in the end he selected the most promising of them and went to work there as one of its brightest prospects for a high level management position.

At One with the Corporate Structure

From the beginning, Martin fitted into the system perfectly. He learned quickly and profited from any errors he made—and he made few. Soon he was the leading contender for promotion among his entire peer group.

Quickly he rose in the hierarchy. He seemed to do nothing wrong. Everyone liked him; people who worked for him were charmed by him; people for whom he worked swore by him. He was one of the golden luminaries of the company.

After some years of continuous success, Martin decided he should strike out on his own. He had learned almost everything there was to learn of the working details of a large company. He thought he should be able to capitalize on his knowledge and start a firm of his own that might even outstrip the giant at which he had learned his trade.

And so after thinking about it for a while, Martin decided to take the plunge and start his own company.

A CASE HISTORY: III

Connie was raised as if there was never such a thing as the Women's Liberation Movement. She accepted that, and married right after high school. She was a nesting type and simply never thought of taking up a profession of any kind. She was bright, but did not fit into the secretarial mold, nor was she eager for a career in teaching or nursing. She grew up oriented to the home; that was the place she understood best.

She loved to cook: meals; snacks; pastries; candies. She had a specialty she had picked up on a trip to Baja California: cactus candy. No one could make it the way she did. It consisted of crystallized cactus pads, with the spikes removed. Connie's version was succulent, sweet, and memorable to anyone who tasted it.

As her circle of friends shrank in the suburb of San Diego where she lived—all her peers were getting jobs and driving off to work every morning with their husbands—Connie found that her contacts were diminishing. It never worried her a bit. She was quite content to work around the house, planning her meals, and doing the housework.

Her husband Craig was a member of the sales force of a manufacturing company. He always did well at his job. The family was financially comfortable and prospered as the children grew up.

Then suddenly a recession struck and a number of large corporations began to merge with others. Consolidation always hurt the employees of the company that was absorbed. Craig's company became part of another company, which in turn was an integral part of a huge international conglomerate. Craig knew that his days were numbered, and he sought work elsewhere.

Unfortunately, all Craig's peers were looking, too. Whatever job openings there were quickly vanished. Craig was not one of the lucky ones who filled those openings. Now Connie's oldest son was eligible for college, but what money the family had been able to put away for him was exhausted during Craig's fruitless quest for work.

When he finally did land a job, it only paid three quarters as much as his previous job had. The oldest boy realized he would have to pay his way through college, but with the colleges also hard-pressed, he was unable to receive a scholarship. Instead he got a job in the shipping room of a San Diego factory.

A neighbor, serving as personnel manager of the company for which Connie's son worked, called her up one day, had lunch with her, and asked her point-blank why she didn't get a job.

"I can't do anything," Connie said in some anguish. "I'm not an employee type."

"You can cook. Nobody cooks anymore. Everybody's too busy working. Cook for them. Make that wonderful cactus candy."

Connie understood the implication. Could she make money cooking? Could she, for example, open up a candy shop? Could she become a professional candy maker and help out with the family income?

Her answer was an emphatic and unequivocal yes! If necessary she could become a businesswoman.

*　　*　　*

Now that we have studied Annette, an alienated, unsuccessful, "impossible" working person; Martin, the perfect, upward motivated "golden boy" of a large organization; and Connie, the home-oriented, nesting housewife, let's see how each fared in their enterprises. Which ones do you think were successful? Which unsuccessful?

A CASE HISTORY: I (CONCLUSION)

Annette's first move was to open up a shop in a crowded seashore resort that flourished only during the summer months. To finance her acquisition, she sold the house in which she and her mother had been living up to her mother's death two years before, and purchased a shop with living quarters attached. Then she moved in and got to work.

Because the shop was in a resort area, she opted to stock curios that would appeal to the visitors of the nearby beaches. She knew nothing about buying for such a shop, but studied her nearby competitors, saw which ones were successful and which ones weren't, and acted accordingly in stocking hers.

The first season business was humdrum, but she managed to stay alive. During the winter months the crowds thinned to a trickle. Annette began to walk up and down the shore in the morning, picking up sea shells, and looking over the flotsam and jetsam that appeared.

In her spare time at the shop she began making art forms out of the shells she had picked up, cementing them together into whatever odd shapes appealed to her. She placed the forms on the counter and forgot about them.

One day one of the few winter customers studied one of the shell forms and asked her how much it cost. Annette was surprised, gave a figure off the top of the head, and the visitor bought the shell form and went off with a smile. Annette found that the second form went almost immediately, and soon her counter was bare.

She gathered more shells, made more forms, and now put price tags on them, letting the price rise as the customers continued to come in and buy. Business next season boomed. She painted faces on some of the shells that didn't have shapes she particularly admired. These went as well as the forms. She continued to scout the shore for shells and made art forms out of them and continued to sell them easily.

One day she brought in a piece of driftwood and was sitting there trying to figure out what to do with it when a customer came in and asked her how much she would sell it for. She immediately quoted a price that might have seemed outrageous to her a year before but did not seem so now. The customer purchased the driftwood and walked out happy.

Soon Annette was supplying art forms by consignment to several of her competitors on the boardwalk. Within two years she had three art-form outlets in various parts of the beach community and was thinking of opening a shop in the middle of the nearest large city.

Within ten years Annette was operating a big-money operation that supplied sea shell art forms, painted sea shells, and driftwood statuettes, cork-float animals, and almost any type of flotsam and jetsam imaginable.

A CASE HISTORY: II (CONCLUSION)

Martin's first move was to open up a clothing shop in a city he had selected after a lot of study and consideration. He wanted everything to be just right, and so he analyzed the consumer profiles of everyone who lived in the areas he was interested in.

He eventually selected an ideal city—not too big, not too small—and searched for the proper shop location. He was going to stock it with men's clothing, as he had always considered himself a person with a feeling for the right kind of clothes, and he was sure this flair would help him succeed.

When he had settled on a shop, easily accessible to the working managerial people he understood so thoroughly, he proceeded to stock it after long and exhaustive observation of the coming styles. He pondered his opening, developing an interesting and exciting promotion campaign of advertising, publicity, and other come-ons.

Writing a Program for Venture Capital

Then he wrote up a detailed business program, pointing out his modus operandi, his rationale for selecting the site, his abilities in corporate management, and so on. A bank immediately put up the money and Martin began purchasing his stock of goods.

The opening came. It was a smash. The shop began operating at full capacity. Martin looked forward to the second year, shopping around for the best buys. The store continued to thrive.

Nevertheless, the bottom line was that the shop continued as it was, but did not *expand*. Martin was disappointed in his inability to follow up his initial success, but continued to work hard and to hope. He treated his help well, using techniques he had mastered at the large corporation for which he had worked. He continued to charm his customers. Everybody was happy.

Reversals and Removals

The third year Martin found that his sales were actually falling off. The people he had attracted to the shop were moving out of the area. Martin went back over all his plans and studied his operation. He knew he must be doing something wrong, but he could find nothing wrong. And yet . . .

What Martin had failed to notice was that he had predicated all his moves on a stable business situation. The part of the city in which he had purchased his shop was in a state of flux, not stability. High city taxes were driving businesses away from the area, the businesses that employed Martin's customers. The clientele he had depended on was simply not there anymore. The usually astute Martin failed to look beyond the tip of his nose. His problem was a simple case of marketing myopia—the inability to intuit what is happening *out of sight*.

By the fifth year Martin was forced to fire half his help. There simply was not enough business. His customers all loved him—those that remained—but there seemed to be no new ones coming in. All around him, the neighborhood was changing. His customers were either being transferred away or leaving town on their own.

Martin was only partly aware of what was happening, and was unable to react to the problem in a positive way. He was too practical-minded, too inured to cause-and-effect, too bound by the books he had read, to come up with a gimmick or bold stroke. When he should have panicked and quit—to start again somewhere else—he simply stuck it out in a vain attempt to succeed by endurance alone.

In the seventh year, Martin sadly closed down his business and went back to work for a corporate giant. Somehow, it was not as easy to succeed at a small business as it was to be part of a large business. At least that was the way it was for Martin.

A CASE HISTORY: III (CONCLUSION)

One of Connie's close friends who lived just down the street was working as an accountant for a profitable grocery store in a nearby shopping mall. When she heard that Connie was thinking about opening a candy shop, she warned her not to do it. Such an operation would be a costly proposition, and Connie would have to pay heavily for rental space in the mall, and perhaps incur a great deal of debt. The overhead, she warned Connie, would be very large.

She suggested that Connie cook cactus candy for the grocery store for which she worked. An interview was arranged, and Connie agreed to a certain amount of the candy for the store for sale each day. The work was easy. In the first several months she worked for the store, Connie was able to produce enough goods on a day-to-day basis to satisfy demand. The candy went fast. Her total income was small, but it helped.

Craig was visiting the store one day on his lunch hour and overheard two women talking about his wife's cactus candy.

"I wish my sister could taste this cactus candy," one of the women said. "She'd love it. But she's back in Detroit where nobody ever heard of it."

"Can't you buy some and mail it to her?" the other woman suggested.

"Why not?"

Craig spent the rest of the day toying with the germ of an idea. Why couldn't Connie sell her cactus candy by mail as well as in the mall? She would still save overhead by not having to open a shop. And the cost of mailing would be borne by the customers.

He spoke to her that night. "If I can generate enough mail orders for you, can you supply the cactus candy to fill them?"

Connie assured him that she could; she had extra time, even with the mall business doing so well.

With his sales expertise, Craig planned and developed a campaign that would advertise Connie's Cactus Candy on an area-wide basis at first. He wrote some unusual and attractive copy, bought small advertising space in regional newspapers and magazines, and wrote direct-mail teasers as well.

24

Suddenly Connie found she couldn't fulfill the orders Craig was bringing in without increasing her cooking space. The space was acquired. Then she found herself spending most of her time supervising two cooks, and then three. Eventually Craig had to quit his job to take over the management of Connie's Candies. Connie added other flavors to her cactus brand, opened a large store in the original mall, branched out into another mall, and was making cactus candy a thing known from one coast to the other.

The point of these case histories is that Annette, with all her false starts, was a born entrepreneur; Martin, with all his marvelous talents and traits, was a born middle manager; and Connie, with her nesting instincts and kitchen-oriented skills, was a born innovator.

People scorned Annette, teachers hated her, management didn't know what to do with her except get rid of her. People loved Martin, wanted him around, couldn't get enough of him. People passed off Connie as if she didn't exist, considered her an out-of-date model in an up-to-date world, and totally ignored her.

Yet when push came to shove, Annette turned out to be an ingenious innovator; Martin turned out to be so set in his ways that he could not change with the times; and Connie turned out to be a hidden dynamo of productivity hiding in the comfortable outer package of a homebody housewife!

What makes an entrepreneur? More importantly, are you the type of person who is cut out to be an entrepreneur? Not everybody is. Certainly there are many more non-entrepreneurs than there are entrepreneurs.

Although business analysts have been studying the subject for some time now, there is really no set answer. There are, however, a number of qualities that help determine who will be a good entrepreneur—and, conversely, a poor entrepreneur. These concern personality, character, attitudes, abilities, psychological makeup, and business background.

Let's take these up one at a time.

THE PERSONALITY OF THE ENTREPRENEUR

The results of a recent study at Baylor University, cited in *Dun's Business Monthly,* demonstrate that the typical successful entrepreneur has a low level of anxiety in his or her makeup, strong abilities along creative lines, generally nonconformist attitudes, an uncanny ability to adapt to change, and an urge to take a chance, no matter what the odds.

In addition to these clearly delineated personality traits, the typical entrepreneur is a person with a high degree of self-confidence, of vision, and with an obsession to be the one in charge, to exert power over others.

According to John Hornaday, a management professor at Babson College:

> [Entrepreneurs] have a low need for support and encouragement, they are usually first-born in their families, and they are increasingly women.

On the other hand, Gustaf Delin, a founder of the ForeSight Institute, a Washington-based venture that helps companies develop in-house entrepreneurs, claims that there absolutely is *not* any perfect list of characteristics that will determine the true entrepreneur. But he does concede one constant:

> Every entrepreneur is self-selected. Nobody appoints you.

In other words, the entrepreneur has, above all else, desire—as well as the need to be independent and to run things in a big way.

Among other qualities, the entrepreneur needs guts, determination, and an extraordinarily high energy level. One entrepreneur believes the most important of all these traits is "fierce dedication to achievement." He goes on to define that as a damn-it-all, I'm-going-to-do-this-if-it-kills-me kind of attitude in the face of insurmountable obstacles. A tremendous sense of self is necessary.

Any entrepreneur must believe fervently in the quality of his or her idea—but most of all must be motivated by a strong desire to make money.

Stamina is basic to the entrepreneur. Good health is essential too. One successful woman entrepreneur puts it this way:

> You can't just do it for a little while and say, "I'm tired." You have to be able to make yourself keep doing it. It's really an endurance race.

It was, she admits, the excitement and fun of it that kept her going during the times when all seemed lost.

THE CHARACTER OF THE ENTREPRENEUR

The entrepreneur must have integrity. Most people who have intensively studied the breed find that integrity is a must for success. If a person involved in starting up an enterprise lacks that single character value, the enterprise will almost certainly fail when the instigator tries something that is unethical or dishonest.

Burt McMurty, a Menlo Park, California, venture capitalist, says:

> Highly ethical people tend not to grasp for strange solutions when they're in trouble.

Most of them he has studied usually don't get along with their supervisors, but are always well liked and respected by employees on their own level, and admired by peers. They usually accept responsibility, make commitments, and stick by them. And they are absolutely honest.

If an entrepreneur is frightened, no one ever knows it, McMurty points out. Many of them have failures before they achieve success, yet they exhibit personal and professional maturity and determination whether or not their venture succeeds.

A key point in the character of the entrepreneur is the orientation to action. Here's what one observer says:

> Entrepreneurs have an action orientation, but it is more than that. They want to *build* something, to *make* something. The pride is in taking a product and making it commercial, in having a new factory and seeing yourself progress. And when guys relax, like ten o'clock at night or something, relaxation is talking about "Do you remember when we started out in that basement or in that garage? And now we've got corporate headquarters and we're building a factory next door." That's the kind of story they tell. It's a pride in building something. I absorbed that atmosphere, and I wanted to give it a try myself.

The CEO of a health-services company says:

> Things like talent, personality, and chemistry are very critical in a small company run by an entrepreneur. In a corporation, one person leaves a job, someone else takes over the position. Everyone seems replaceable.

Not so in a smaller company. Says another venture capitalist:

> An entrepreneur is a builder and yet a dreamer. The entrepreneur should reach for the moon, but keep the feet on the ground.

This means being realistic about all things at all times, being optimistic but not wildly over-optimistic. The successful entrepreneur is not a bee flitting about from one bud to another—although many people mistakenly picture the entrepreneur as just such a person—but must be tough-minded and sure of purpose.

Another characteristic the entrepreneur should have is

the ability to improvise, if necessary, to change course in midstream. The entrepreneur must be able to take criticism well, to be thick-skinned when necessary. Not every venture an entrepreneur takes on will succeed, so such a person must be impervious to discouragement. However, the entrepreneur must equally guard against misplaced Pollyannaish optimism.

Boredom must also be endured at times. Mostly, though, the entrepreneur must act. One in the middle of the long, hard ascent to success puts it thus:

> But whether I make it or not, the important thing is that I put my arms around something and brought it to life.

Says Doug Greene, an entrepreneur who made it publishing a natural foods trade journal:

> You can read all the books about swimming, you can see films about it, you can sit on the bank and watch, but until you dive in that water, you don't know how to swim. That's what entrepreneurs do. They dive into the water, and they learn how to swim.

THE ATTITUDES OF THE ENTREPRENEUR

The most important attitude of the entrepreneur is an imperviousness to the fear of danger. The successful achiever must have, above all, an outlook on life that allows him or her to take a risk on something that may prove disastrous if it goes wrong. The entrepreneur must have a sense of daring and be willing to take the big gamble.

Yet the ability to take a risk should not be mistaken for a headlong plunge into sure ruin. The kind of risk the entrepreneur takes is a *calculated* risk, the kind of chance that usually will come out a winner. The entrepreneur does not exhibit—nor should exhibit—the type of risk-taking the inveterate gambler takes. Psychologists point out that the gambler *wants* to lose; the entrepreneur wants to win.

The Psychology of Risk

There is a subtle difference here, made clear by a recent psychological test. A study was performed on a group of entrepreneurs who had left their jobs to start new businesses, on a second group of employees who had joined large companies recently, and on a third group who had been promoted within their organization.

Each member of the test groups was encouraged to imagine that he or she had just inherited $4,000 and could choose between investment in stable blue-chip mutual funds, or speculation in a new company. The money might double in two years if the company succeeded, but the person could lose the entire $4,000 if the company failed. How good do the odds need to be for the person to invest: a three in ten chance? a five in ten chance? a seven in ten chance?

In this question, there was little difference between the entrepreneurs and the other workers. About two thirds of both groups were "moderate" risk-takers, choosing to speculate in the new company if the odds reached five to seven in ten.

Unhappy in Your Work?

In another question, each person was asked about job satisfaction. The entrepreneurs revealed that they were significantly more unhappy with the jobs they had just left than the people in the other groups. Eagerness to escape, not eagerness to take a chance, was a major impetus to become an entrepreneur.

Job dissatisfaction not only starts new businesses, the psychologist discovered, but it keeps them going. Entrepreneurs who scored highest in job dissatisfaction were still in business four years later. The less dissatisfied entrepreneurs were no longer in business. That is, the entrepreneurs who succeeded were no more prone to risk-taking than those who failed; but the entrepreneurs who succeeded were far more dissatisfied with their previous jobs than those who generally failed.

The point is an important one: it is not always the psychological pattern of taking the risk that counts, but the *reason* for taking the risk in the first place.

THE ABILITIES OF THE ENTREPRENEUR

Among the many abilities the entrepreneur should possess are several important ones:

- ❏ The ability to formulate a good idea.
- ❏ The ability to select an idea with growth potential.
- ❏ The ability to understand and control finances.
- ❏ The ability to concentrate.
- ❏ The ability to sacrifice oneself totally for a specific enterprise.
- ❏ The ability to give up all personal comfort for a career.

The ability to formulate a good idea is essential to the entrepreneur. A product or a service must fill a special need and be good enough to fill a niche not yet filled by anything else.

Venture capital partner Jacqueline Morby of Boston explains:

It has to have an aspect to differentiate it from other products on the market. Ideas must have

31

what is called "real economic potential." That is, they must be able to stick and not fade out like a fad within months.

The ability to select an idea with growth potential is equally as important.

Andrew S. Grove, president of Intel Corporation of Santa Clara, California, says:

> It's like an artist. He can envision a statue or a painting by staring at nothing. In the same sense, a person who creates a business or product does so by looking at a blank canvas.

Then, if the entrepreneur trusts that vision enough, he or she finally shows the world that the image that he or she saw is *real*.

The ability to understand and control finances is also essential for the entrepreneur. He or she must have a natural ability to juggle resources without getting into complicated difficulties. There is a kind of creative genius in moving money around in the right way to cover sudden gaps and have enough when a crisis demands it. Entrepreneurship is basically focused on the acquisition of money and the ability to make money do any kind of dance the dance-master wants it to do.

The real purpose and focus of the entrepreneur is on the money and not the product, the service, or even the customer. It is sometimes difficult for a person to see this, especially someone who has been brought up in a comfortable, affluent economy during a time of prosperity when love of money is something to hide under the carpet—but it is nevertheless important to understand.

The ability to concentrate is a primary need. One venture capitalist puts it this way:

> Those people have an unusual ability to focus for long periods on one or two important things, excluding the rest.

He goes on to say:

> There's an inaccurate characterization of entrepreneurs being full of ideas and flying like a

bee from one flower to another. That's not how they are.

Actually, the entrepreneur is almost obsessed by his or her one product or service. A person who is unable to concentrate all vitality, energy, and intelligence on a specific target for a long period of time, in spite of all the odds against it, should not try to be an entrepreneur; he or she lacks the principal active ingredient for success.

Another important ability is that of being able to sacrifice one's comfortable life-style for the sake of a specific enterprise. Says one entrepreneur:

> Family life comes second. The object is success, and that means being evangelical about it. I once sat down with the wife of an entrepreneur and she told me he'd missed her birthday, Thanksgiving, the birth of a child, their tenth anniversary—she went through the whole bit.

And yet the entrepreneur is not a workaholic. The workaholic does not make a total sacrifice to an ideal such as a product or a service; rather, the workaholic works in order to escape from personal ties and personal problems elsewhere. It is the motivation that differentiates the entrepreneur and his or her total sacrifice from the workaholic who must escape from personal problems that have proved overwhelming.

One female entrepreneur puts it this way:

> You do not have time to exert any mental effort in any direction other than your business. So if you are trying to build an emotional relationship, you can't do it. One or the other has to fail—either your relationship or your business. You have to be happy with either fidelity or celibacy.

THE PSYCHOLOGICAL MAKEUP OF THE ENTREPRENEUR

One student of business who runs a school for entrepreneurs in Tarrytown, New York, describes the average entrepreneur as basically an alienated person. Says Robert L. Schwartz:

> You may be an outsider, a special breed of cat, but there's a socially useful, personally useful pattern to that—the world needs nuts like you.

He refers to entrepreneurs generally as "poets and packagers of new ideas." But in the case of the successful entrepreneur, that alienation has prodded him or her into becoming a successful initiator of a new business venture.

Another facet of alienation is the desire to work independently, to work alone. One woman who specializes in business start-ups says that the potential entrepreneur should ask himself or herself this question before going out on his or her own:

> If I had a choice of earning twice as much working for someone else, would I still rather be my own boss?

The true entrepreneur, she says, will always answer that question with a resounding yes!

One successful entrepreneur who started a microcomputer hardware and software company on $25,000 and built it into a $50 million company agrees and says that it was not money that motivated her:

> No. It's a great scorecard. The bottom line tells you yes, it was a success, or no, it wasn't. But money is not a main motivator.

This woman's motivation was something else entirely:

> I had worked for a number of other people and didn't feel that I was always appreciated or got to do many of the things I was capable of doing.

In fact, she wanted to do it herself, and to do it better.

Which brings up another important point in the profile of the entrepreneur. No matter what it is, the entrepreneur simply wants *to do it better*. It's not perfectionism so much as it is the desire to get something done in a more effective way.

A venture capitalist who has financed many successful entrepreneurs puts it this way:

> Entrepreneurs have quite a bit in common with artists, not the least of which is the desire to do some one thing extremely well.

Richard Boyatzis, of McBer & Co., says about entrepreneurs:

> They always have a desire to do better—to improve on the previous performance. They are never satisfied.

And there is also a need for recognition—the kind of recognition that corporations rarely give their employees. Most entrepreneurs are self-motivated, and proud of themselves, almost to a fault:

> We perceive ourselves as agents of our own success or failure, and failure, to us, is having to work for someone else. Still, there isn't one of us who doesn't, at times, think we'd be wise to rejoin the comfort of a structured organization. Some of us do, occasionally, but most of us feel, most of the time, that the trade-off isn't worth it.

So says Jane Adams, author of *Making Good: Conversations with Successful Men*.

THE BUSINESS BACKGROUND OF
THE ENTREPRENEUR

One of the things the average entrepreneur must possess to be successful is experience in the business world, usually within the protective walls of a large company. In fact, it is learning the tricks of the trade in a large company, so to speak, that does the potential entrepreneur the most good. By understanding the traps and perils of corporate existence, the entrepreneur will know the ropes ahead of time. By developing a specific expertise to avoid these pitfalls, the entrepreneur then trains himself or herself to be an expert in maneuvering out of the corporate labyrinth.

Nevertheless, working for a small company can give an entrepreneur a lot more broad-based experience. A partner in a venture capital firm says:

> You become attuned to what small-company demands are. It's much more hectic.

Either way, the entrepreneur needs to know how business works so he or she can make it work for himself or herself.

3

Finding Your Entrepreneurial Quotient

It's always difficult to decide whether to go out on your own or to take a chance on making good in business in a big way. Because few people really know if they have the right stuff to make good entrepreneurs, it's wise to look into your own motivations and desires to find out if you even have the basic wish to do so.

Once you've settled that vital question, then comes the acid test. You should really check up on yourself to see if you're the right psychological type to be a successful entrepreneur. There's no use trying to be a concert singer if you just don't have the voice.

How can you determine your E.Q.—your entrepreneurial quotient?

The following fourteen questions have been devised as a self-help test to allow you to find out for yourself. In taking the E.Q. test, select the answer that seems most likely to fit the question *in its entirety*. Circle (A), (B), or (C) to indicate your answer. When you have finished answering all fourteen questions, look at the end of the chapter for the proper answers, and give yourself one point for every question you answered correctly. A score of fourteen indicates you are the perfect type for an entrepreneur. A score of ten indicates that you might well make the grade. A score of six indicates you might have trouble.

Even if you score six or below, that doesn't mean you can't apply yourself to the job of being your own boss—but it does mean that you should pay a great deal of attention to the material offered in this book. It will help you over the many pitfalls and trouble spots on the way.

When you have finished determining your score, go on to read the discussion that follows to learn the essential differences between the various selections, and finding out why the "best" answer is considered the best and what its selection, or nonselection, by you means in the evaluation of your own entrepreneurial profile.

YOUR ENTREPRENEURIAL QUOTIENT

(1) To succeed at any undertaking, it is much more important:

(A) to set a proper goal or objective before beginning.

(B) to shift ground quickly when you realize that you are losing.

(C) to set a goal and stick to it no matter what happens.

(2) In order to insure effective performance in any act it is necessary:

(A) to make sure each performance is satisfactory in every detail.

(B) to make sure each performance is an improvement over the previous one.

(C) to make sure each performance is as good as it possibly can be.

(3) To succeed at any particular task it is mandatory:

(A) to do the job slowly and with determination.

(B) to find out all you can about the job before you attempt it.

(C) to make sure you do the job with the least amount of waste motion.

(4) If you are entrusted to execute a dangerous mission the first thing to do is:

(A) make sure your course of action is thoroughly foolproof.

(B) take as many calculated risks as possible to insure success.

(C) proceed with caution, intelligence, and determination.

(5) In choosing a person as a role model for your own actions, you would select:

(A) a person who is in complete control of his or her destiny.

(B) a person of impeccable determination, taste, understanding, and bearing.

(C) a person who can grasp hold of power and then know exactly how to wield it.

(6) If you have a choice of selecting one of three paths you would choose:

(A) the shortest, quickest, and simplest trail to the eventual goal.

(B) the winding trail that encounters beautiful and serene country to the eventual goal.

(C) the slippery trail that encounters dangerous rocks, landslides, and peril to the eventual goal.

(7) You're proud of your job history, which includes:

(A) a long tenure at an important job in a large, successful firm.

(B) a series of short-lived jobs that have moved you steadily upward.

(C) a history of being fired from important jobs more than once.

(8) In your family you are:

(A) the last-born child.

(B) the middle-born child.

(C) the first-born child.

(9) In your daily on-the-job working experience, you:

(A) like working for people who know what they are doing.

(B) hate working for people who turn out to be fools and boors.

(C) hate working for *anybody*.

(10) In a complicated business situation that demands the proper approach you would rather:

(A) work with a business partner or colleague who is a good friend and can be trusted.

(B) work with a colleague who has already shown talent and resourcefulness and can be trusted.

(C) work with an expert who is a total stranger and about whose personal habits nothing is known.

(11) Your choice for the best right-hand man or woman is always:

    (A) a person who is bright, talented, imaginative, and energetic.

    (B) a person who is dull, plodding, but honest and uncompromising.

    (C) a person who is brilliant, conceited, self-centered, but noncompetitive.

(12) When you gamble you:

    (A) always bet on a sure thing.

    (B) always bet on a long shot.

    (C) always bet across the board.

(13) In a dangerous and critical situation that may end up fatally you try:

    (A) to stick to the commendable, honorable, and decent way out.

    (B) to come up with a brilliant stroke that will free you from trouble.

    (C) to improvise your way out of the difficulty one cautious step at a time.

(14) Do you think that the best way to succeed in any kind of business undertaking is:

    (A) to work hard.

    (B) to work smart.

    (C) to work hard and smart.

ANSWERS TO THE E.Q. TEST

(1)	(C)	(8)	(C)
(2)	(B)	(9)	(C)
(3)	(B)	(10)	(C)
(4)	(B)	(11)	(C)
(5)	(A)	(12)	(A)
(6)	(A)	(13)	(C)
(7)	(C)	(14)	(C)

REVIEW OF THE QUESTIONS

QUESTION #1:

Although it is necessary to shift ground quickly when you realize you are losing in an undertaking, the really important thing is for you to have a habit of setting a goal and sticking to it no matter what happens during the rough and tumble. It is the persistent, determined, and no-nonsense person who is going to succeed at independent work—no matter what happens around him or her.

QUESTION #2:

The successful entrepreneur will always try to top one performance by a *better* one. Nothing satisfies the true entrepreneur. Looking back on a performance, the entrepreneur will see a half a dozen things that should have been done better. The next time such an effort is attempted, the entrepreneur will make sure the job is done better.

QUESTION #3:

Investigation into a situation beforehand is one of the most important preliminaries to the successful conclusion of an effort. A rash gambler may rush into a wager without looking at it beforehand, although most gamblers at least test the waters first. The trained athlete or professional businessperson never goes into anything without knowing as much as possible about what is there waiting for him or her.

QUESTION #4:

Although most entrepreneurs proceed with caution, intelligence, and determination, that is not the point of the question. To take a "calculated" risk is not to leap before you look. It is making a judgment based on what risks are to your advantage and your disadvantage. It is indeed the calculated risk that is in your favor; that is the one that should be taken.

QUESTION #5:

For the entrepreneur, being in complete control of his or her destiny is the crucial point in being a sole proprietor. Although taste, impeccable discrimination, understanding, and bearing are important in a role model, these characteristics are secondary to the entrepreneur. So also is the ability to grasp power and know how to wield it secondary to the main concept of being in control of one's own destiny.

QUESTION #6:

The entrepreneur is primarily concerned with the final goal or objective. Setting that goal and steering toward it regardless of obstacles or distractions is the name of the game. Thus, once the goal is set, the entrepreneur will take the easiest and simplest way to get to that goal.

QUESTION #7:

One key factor in the entrepreneur's motivation to do a job himself or herself is dissatisfaction with working conditions on the job for someone else. The entrepreneur's job history is not going to be one of long and successful tenure in a job well done; it is going to be a series of firings because of continual dissatisfaction. Nor is the person who moves steadily from job to job on the way upward necessarily a potential entrepreneur; he or she is probably someone who understands the game of corporate maneuver and is happy to be playing it.

QUESTION #8:

Statistics show that the more successful entrepreneurial type is usually the first-born in a family. For some reason, there are psychological reasons that the first-born strives more, works smarter, learns the ropes faster, and generally is able to succeed better than others in the line. Naturally, the first-born does not necessarily become the entrepreneur—but the roots are there.

QUESTION #9:

The key word in this question is "for"—"working *for* people." The true entrepreneur never wants to work *for* anyone else. He or she wants to work strictly on his or her own to accomplish what he or she wants. For the entrepreneur, there is no satisfaction in doing something well for someone else. The only satisfaction is in accomplishing on his or her own. And so the entrepreneur can be said always to hate working for *anybody*.

QUESTION #10:

People who lead sheltered business lives and like to be sheltered in the work force always prefer to work with others who are well known to them. It is the entrepreneur only who never really cares with whom he or she is working, as long as that person is an expert on a subject, and knows exactly how to do it. The person who must always seek out someone who can be trusted is not a person who can make decisions and maneuver through the business world with all its rough and tumble situations and with all its people who may prove to be untrustworthy. In addition, colleagues of long standing sometimes tend to become sloppy and self-satisfied; without intending to do so, they may let you down.

QUESTION #11:

The entrepreneur usually chooses brilliant people to work for him or her—not a person who is dull, plodding, but honest. Nevertheless, the entrepreneur understands enough about human nature not to choose a brilliant person who is energetic or hyperactive. Such people tend to sap the strength of all those around them. The entrepreneur needs his or her own energy to move himself or herself and his or her projects; he or she cannot allow a hyperactive colleague to neutralize that energy and allow the project to lose steam and founder. Thus the entrepreneur's ideal associate would be a brilliant and knowledgeable—but noncompetitive—person.

QUESTION #12:

Although it might seem that the entrepreneur, being in a risk-taking business, might bet the long shot to come in, it is not the case. An inveterate gambler bets the long shot because the inveterate gambler usually wants to lose. Nor does the entrepreneur bet across the board. Betting across the board tends to cut down the eventual winnings, to diminish the final take. The entrepreneur finds the sure thing after considerable study and investigation of an imaginative nature—and bets on that.

QUESTION #13:

The magic word in the entrepreneur's modus operandi is "improvisation." It is not the brilliant stroke that frees the entrepreneur from trouble, but it is the ability to improvise and act one step at a time to work out of a dangerous spot that differentiates the entrepreneur from all others. The commendable, honorable, and decent way out of a difficulty generally lands that person in a situation roughly comparable to "back to square one." That's all right for the dull plodder, or the person who luxuriates in the corporate structure, but it is anathema to the born entrepreneur.

QUESTION #14:

This is not really a tricky question, although it might seem to be. To work hard is to put a great deal of energy into a project. For the average person, working hard seems enough in itself. It is good to work hard—that is the essence of the work ethic. Nevertheless, it is really not enough. To work smart is to be totally effective—successful—at one particular phase of an operation. To work smart also carries with it a connotation of working deviously and close to the ethical edge. But to work smart is actually to be totally effective and efficient in an operation. In itself, to work smart is not enough, either. One who works smart is finished upon achievement of a particular sub-goal. It's over when the goal is reached. The entrepreneur knows the value of both operations. The entrepreneur therefore works hard *and* works smart. Working smart gets the small goals out of the way quickly, opening up more hard work for the entrepreneur. Working hard and working smart become a chain reaction for the entrepreneur. It is the secret of achievement *and* consolidation.

4

Spotting a Need and Filling It

A CASE HISTORY

When the container company Jim worked for as a member of middle management was merged into a larger shipping firm, he managed to survive on the job for six months, but was finally terminated after the usual shakeup in the middle executive levels.

He had trouble getting himself resettled. Other middle managers who had worked with him were also looking for work. After many seasons of prosperity and affluence, middle management was suddenly the place not to be.

Jim continued his weekly tennis matches with his friend Ray, an accountant for a firm that manufactured television antennas. The tennis courts were located at a country club in a rural area of the community. Every Saturday on the way to their weekly matches, the two of them stopped at a small crossroads store to fill up on gas and buy snacks for lunch.

The store was the only one in that remote area. A typical mom-and-pop operation, run by an elderly husband and wife, it was busy on Saturdays. Yet the owners did not hire extra help to cope with the extra influx of customers or make any attempt to stock supplies that would normally be purchased by weekend tourists.

An Idea Off the Top of the Head

One morning Ray was particularly annoyed at the length of time he had to stand in line to buy a packet of cheese nips and cookies. When he rejoined Jim he mentioned the fact that the couple was missing an opportunity to make a good thing out of the store. What it needed was some more gas pumps, a little added room for more groceries, and maybe a coffee takeout counter.

Their tennis game was rained out that afternoon, and as the two friends drove back home they began to discuss the little store. Jim needed work, and Ray could always use a little extra income. If the two of them could get up enough money to purchase the store, Jim could run it and Ray could help out in his spare time.

That same day they drove back to the store and found it deserted because of the rainy weather. They sat down with the owners and talked about the possibility of buying the property from them. It turned out that the couple had been trying to think of some way to close down the place because it was getting to be too much of a hassle for them.

Getting into Business

Ray mentioned a price he thought was fair to buy the store, and found to his surprise the couple was interested. After some more discussion, Jim and Ray found that the couple would be glad to let the place go for the sum mentioned. Ray wrote out a check for a deposit on a forth-

48

coming down payment. The couple was instructed to make a full inventory of the store and its facilities; then final settlement would be made and a contract of sale drawn up.

On the way home, Ray agreed to put up the lion's share of the purchase price, with the stipulation that Jim would pay him back as he got enough money to do so. At home Jim mentioned the purchase of the store to his wife. She told him that she liked the idea very much and would speak to her parents, now retired and in Florida. Soon she obtained enough money to pay half the purchase price, and Jim and Ray were in business without Jim's obligation to pay back a big loan.

Refurbishing the Premises

In six weeks the couple sold the store and moved to California. Jim allocated himself a regular salary out of the normal day-to-day proceeds of the store and began spending his time rebuilding the interior, restocking the merchandise, and waiting on the few customers who happened by during the week.

Ray was busy on weekends, checking over the receipts, paying the bills, and keeping financial records. At the same time, he helped out at the gas pumps and at the counter. Jim's wife and children came by in the afternoons during the week to help out.

Although there was not a lot of business right at first, within six months people began to stop in for the various new items now stocked on their way home or on their way into the country. Jim added a takeout counter, where he served coffee and sandwiches for the sportsmen who came to the area for its hunting and fishing.

By the time a year had passed, the store had doubled in size. It now carried a full line of groceries and sundries. Two gas pumps were added for a total of three. Jim built a lean-to shed and stocked automobile products for the do-it-yourself mechanic. He also added a section inside the store catering to sports enthusiasts, offering back-packing equipment, hiking boots, overnight shelter rigs, and other sporting goods.

The partners celebrated the end of the year by forming a corporation with several other members of their families; the object was to obtain more operating capital. Jim found the store hours long and physically exhausting, but he kept at it to improve the place.

Expanding the Existing Facilities

One day as Jim was driving along the road into town for a visit to the bank, he noticed a sign announcing the division of a large section of land into small tracts for houses. That afternoon he was on the phone to Ray.

There was a ten-acre section of undeveloped former farmland across the road from the store and the two were able to purchase it for a very good price. Jim drew up plans for a newer, larger store—including a bakery department, a delicatessen, a meat market, and a vegetable and produce department. He also had an idea that he could build a garage next to the store, and hire mechanics to service cars.

Both Jim and Ray began poking around in the city, asking questions of food wholesalers, and making tours of large retail stores and supermarkets to get all the information they could about general merchandising. Putting as much of their newly absorbed know-how into the plans for their store and garage, they approached a bank to ask for money to build the facilities.

In a series of frustrating and disappointing interviews, they were turned down.

Financing for the Enterprise

Finally the two decided to put up all they owned as collateral and take out a loan from a commercial bank. That was the only way they could get the money. Within ten months, the new store was constructed and open for business.

Meanwhile the tract of new residences was expanding, and another one was projected for an area out past Jim and Ray's store. Now business really began booming as people started to move into the first development and others began driving by to investigate the new area. Business volume grew dramatically as both sections prospered and the population expanded.

Ray is now chairman of the board of a well-established corporation. The firm owns six supermarket operations and is now planning the first shopping center in the area. But the same original five owners now operate three other affiliated corporations they own, including rental projects, real estate firms, and buildings in the city. They are millionaires. Self-made.

Of course, this may seem like a Horatio Alger story, but it is nothing of the kind. It is simply a matter of need, ingenuity, and energy. Ray was the focal point of the operation. As an accountant, he knew business principles, cash flow, and financial matters. Jim, the middle-level manager, learned quickly, and adapted his skills to building and selling in the retail area. Both men sought out information from others when they needed it.

The point is, each man used his own strong suit to help create what turned out to be a large corporate empire. But before being able to put his strong suit to use each had to tap his imagination and intelligence to see clearly an opportunity that could not be passed by. In effect, Jim and Ray recognized the need for a store in the area where they played tennis—and their answer was to *fill the need.*

That was the key to their success.

FILLING A NEED—OR CREATING A NEED

There is obviously another side to the coin labeled *fill the need*. For every entrepreneur who has observed a need, studied it, and established a means of filling the need, there is another entrepreneur who has identified a particular talent or skill he or she has, and has had the intuitive flair to market the skill by *creating a need* for it.

Of course, sometimes creating a need is simply another way of looking at filling a need. There are consumers out there with an undeveloped or unknown need for a product or service. The entrepreneur *recognizes* that unknown need, and makes it known to the buyer. Although this is in part the psychology of salesmanship, it is something else again in the creation of a need.

One of the most important talents the entrepreneur boasts of is a skill in sensing accurately the needs and desires of people who might be potential purchasers—of a product or service that they do not even know about. To elaborate, the entrepreneur not only understands the psychological motivation of the individual buyer, but the motivation of the *whole marketplace of collective buyers*.

Market Research on the Cuff

The truth of the matter is that the entrepreneur does not deal intuitively all the time. There comes that moment after the initial flash of inspiration has run its course, and the entrepreneur must devise practical solutions to the new problems confronting him or her. But the *sensing* mechanism continues. Sensing public merchandising needs is simply an exercise in market research on an individual basis.

While big companies have hundreds of people involved in market research, the entrepreneur usually depends on his or her own sensitivity. You can accomplish investigative research of this kind simply by looking around and studying the people you see.

Let's assume for the moment that you are going to pursue a kind of investigative market research to determine what might be a possible need in the public at large. In a way, this is really putting the cart before the horse; but for the sake of illustration, it may be the easiest way to approach the problem.

The idea is to examine a market area in depth, and develop a profile of it. That means you should try to find out what type of people live in a particular area, what kind of jobs they have, what their income is, how their housing differs, and what their life-styles are. These are intimate details, of course, but they are important if you are going to understand the area where you intend to set up a business.

The Six Basic Points

The Small Business Administration, a group formed by the federal government to help out sole proprietors and small-business operators, says that there are six important points you should know about people you want to do business with:

❑ general characteristics of the population

❑ social characteristics of the population

❑ labor force characteristics of the population

❑ income characteristics of the population

❑ occupancy, utilization, and financial characteristics of housing units

❑ structural, equipment, and financial characteristics of housing units

You can find these six facts by looking at the *Census Bureau of Population and Housing,* published by the U.S. Chamber of Commerce and Bureau of Census. In fact, the Bureau of Census has divided these reports into the six points mentioned above for all parts of the country. These regions are called Standard Metropolitan Statistical Areas (SMSA).

The reports are further subdivided to reflect the characteristics of specific locations in and around each SMSA, each location having a population of at least 50,000. This breakdown enables you to zero in on any community in order to determine the facts applying to that area.

Then if you assemble all these facts, you can determine details of information about any part of the country's population that might come in handy for you in your proposed business:

❏ age by sex

❏ persons per household

❏ nationality

❏ educational attainment

❏ employment status

❏ occupation

❏ family income

❏ income source

❏ number of homes owned

❏ number of homes
(apartments) rented

❏ number of people per housing unit

❏ value of housing

❏ size of housing

It's a game of detection. You find the average number of people in a household in the section on general characteristics of the population.

Then you find nationality and educational attainment in the section on social characteristics of the population.

Then you find the employment status and occupation in the section on labor force characteristics of the population.

Then you find the number of homes owned and the number of homes rented in the section on occupancy, utilization, and financial characteristics of housing units.

There is even an overview of many of these facts in a book titled *Urban Atlas Tract Data for SMSA*, published by the Department of Commerce.

What to Do with a Profile

Let's take a look at a typical profile that might emerge in a quick study of a particular "tract" in SMSA. The profile might look like this:

Number of families	795
Number of families with income of about $10,000 a year	198
Number of automobiles available per housing unit, two autos or less	325
Median value of one-family house	$6,500

In turn, this picture can give you a pretty fair idea of the kind of people who live in that particular community. And it can give you a pretty fair picture of the consumer you might be trying to attract.

A Little Investigative Research

Research is never limited to one quick overview—especially with second-hand information. If you want to know in detail about the people who live in a certain area, there are many other ways to find out how many automobiles a family has, how much income it makes, and how much the real estate is worth.

You can use visual research—really the best kind of all and the only kind that cannot be faulted, because it is first-hand information. By taking a drive through a neighborhood you can see for yourself the number of cars. You can see for yourself the way the houses look. You can see their size, their condition—well-kept or ill-kept—and their style.

You can also use personal research—getting out and talking to people in a neighborhood. It's sometimes this kind of investigation of an area that tells you whether you are going to have much of a chance of building a good business in a particular neighborhood. It's sometimes a specific personal investigation of an area that tells the intelligent entrepreneur whether he or she has a chance to make a go of a certain kind of shop or venture in that specific place.

In Search of a Business

We've already looked at one aspect of opening a business—the examination of specific neighborhoods or communities to find out where a business can succeed. There's another important aspect not yet covered. Let's suppose, for example, you want to open a business in a place you have already selected and are familiar with, but don't know what kind of business to start. This is a familiar problem with many would-be entrepreneurs.

The way to approach this aspect of the problem is the counterpart of the first approach. That is, you must sit down and try to figure out what kind of business would be best for a particular area and what kind of business would fulfill a need there.

To search out a business you might begin by asking yourself a number of questions about the neighborhood. For example:

QUESTION #1

What kind of business would best fit your own special skills, interests, hopes, and dreams?

QUESTION #2

What type of business is unavailable in the community at the present time, and why is it unavailable? Was it, in fact, available at one time? If so, what happened?

QUESTION #3

Exactly what do people in the community really need and really want at the present time?

QUESTION #4

How much would it cost for you to provide a service that seems to be needed in the community?

QUESTION #5

What kind of licenses, official approvals, changes in zoning, permits, accounting or bookkeeping services, or extra help will you need if you decide to open a business?

QUESTION #6

Are there any services that people of the community would be willing to pay for if they could get them? If so, what are they?

QUESTION #7

If you were to start up a particular business in this community, how much money would you need up front to allow for a certain number of months when no money will come in to put back into the business?

QUESTION #8

Do the chances look good that if you did open a business in the community you would make a fair profit on it?

QUESTION #9

If so, how much profit would there be allocated to you after all your costs have been figured out? Would it be enough for you?

Services Most Communities Need

In looking for a specific type of service or product to fill a need in a community, you should always keep in mind a general overall list of such services so that if a need becomes evident, you will be able immediately to plug in a particular service or product.

As a memory jogger, here is an extensive list, broken up into various segments, naming services that you might provide for any community.

The general service areas are:

❏ business service

❏ community service

❏ educational service

❏ entertainment service

❏ health service

❏ maintenance service

❏ personal service

❏ pet service

❏ transportation service

❏ tool rental service

❏ sports service

BUSINESS SERVICE

Accounting
Advertising
Appraising
Auctioneering
Banking
Bookkeeping
Credit and collection
Delivery
Data processing
Duplicating
Employment agency
Income tax preparation
Investment counseling
Office equipment repair
Printing
Photography
Secretarial help
Scrap recycling
Sign painting
Telephone answering
Writing

COMMUNITY SERVICE

Appliance repair
Art gallery
Auto repair
Car wash
Dating service
Dry cleaning
Funeral home
Hauling
Hotel/motel
Insurance agent
Laundromat
Newspaper delivery
Photography
Real estate agent
Travel agent

EDUCATIONAL SERVICE

Acting school
Art gallery
Craft instruction
Language instruction
Literary agent
Martial arts school
Modeling school
Musical instruction
Newsletter
Newspaper
Pollster
Researcher
Tutor
Vehicle driving school
Writer
Yoga instruction

ENTERTAINMENT SERVICE

Amusement park
Catering service
Cinema operator
Dance studio
Entertainer
Event promoter
Filmmaker
Piano tuner
Riding stable
Talent agent
Writer

HEALTH SERVICE

Convalescent home
Companion for shut-ins
Dentist
Dietician
Health club

Meals for shut-ins
Nurse
Physician
Psychiatrist/psychologist
Rehabilitation therapist
Transportation of handicapped
Wheelchair rental

MAINTENANCE SERVICE

Air conditioning maintenance
Carpenter
Chimney sweep
Electrician
Floor, rug, drape cleaning
Furnace maintenance
Hotel/motel maintenance
Interior decorator
Lawn care, landscaping
Painting, exterior and interior
Pest control
Plant and garden maintenance
Plumber
Refuse removal
Security
Snow removal
Swimming pool maintenance
Television repair
Window washing

PERSONAL SERVICE

Babysitter
Butler
Cook
Chauffeur
Family financial counselor
Haircutting and stylist
Home cleaning

Income tax preparation
Laundry and ironing
Manicurist
Shopping service
Special event telephone alert
Telephone wakeup
Travel agents
Upholsterer

PET SERVICE

Boarding
Dog walking
Grooming
Training
Veterinarian

TRANSPORTATION SERVICE

Bus
Car rental
Chartered aircraft
Parking lot
Railroad
Taxi
Trailer rental
Truck rental

TOOL RENTAL SERVICE

Agricultural equipment
Air compressor
Construction equipment
Generators
Sump pump
Hand tools

SPORTS SERVICE

Billiard parlor
Bowling alley
Campgrounds
Golf course
Hockey rink
Roller-skating rink
Skateboard court
Sports equipment rental
Sports training school
Tennis and racquetball court

5

Getting the
Money

A CASE HISTORY

Jennifer and Bob had always wanted to open up a bookstore and run it in partnership, but both had worked full-time since their marriage. When their two children finally reached high school age, they decided to take a chance and do what they had always wanted to do.

They were aware that television viewing had been cutting into book sales for a number of years, but they were lucky enough to live in a community on the outskirts of a metropolitan area where the pace was less hectic and where there were only a handful of television channels available for watching.

There was also the fact that the particular town where they lived—an old, well-established, and comfortable community dating back two hundred years or more—had no existing bookstore. In fact, their own children had often groused about having to drive twenty miles to buy records and tape cassettes—and the occasional book.

The Necessary Background Experience

Jennifer was particularly suited to a career of selecting books for people to read. She had served as a librarian in the tiny local library and had then taken a job as the head librarian in the town's school system. Bob worked for the county as an engineer. They owned a home in the center of town, a home that was of course mortgaged and not yet paid off.

In spite of their tight financial situation caused by the bringing up and educating of their two children, they had managed to save a few thousand dollars and had carefully squirreled it away for future use. Now the time had come. They would use the money to start their venture.

They had even finally come to a decision about exactly what the store would feature. It would be a shop dealing predominantly in books, hardbacks and paperbacks, suitable to the community in which they lived. In addition to books, the store would sell records and tape cassettes, items their children always wished were on sale nearer home.

In addition, Jennifer had a green thumb and felt she could stock and sell plants to townsfolk who were enthusiastic about her own garden successes. As a sideline, they decided to sell unpainted furniture in kit form, for Bob was something of an expert on finishing furniture.

The Old Problem of Money

The big challenge was money. Jennifer and Bob figured they would need enough capital to carry the shop for at least six months before they would reach the break-even point. That sum included necessities like rent, a little promotion, supplies, telephone, electricity, maintenance, and some renovations, although Bob could make most of the changes himself. At present, they only had half of what they needed to get themselves safely started.

They decided to try for a business loan from their own bank. They knew, of course, that if that failed, they would always be able to take out a personal loan. But if they were forced to do that, the amount they could take out would be cut in half, and that would not be enough to give them a comfortable margin of safety.

Ways to Finance a New Venture

In looking around they found they could finance their shop in two different ways: by debt financing and by equity financing.

In debt financing, they could borrow cash, paying back the amount plus interest as soon as the money was earned. By using the debt-financing method, they would still own and control their entire business.

In equity financing, they could sell shares in the proposed business to individuals, giving them a portion of control and potential profits in return for the cash to start up the business. Shares of stock or shares of partnership could be involved in such a transaction. Of course, they would not be able to control the business or own it fully; the profits likewise would be divided with others.

They also learned that they could always take out a passbook loan, borrowing money against the amount they had in their savings account, using the savings as collateral. But that would give them only half the amount they needed. They could even take out a personal loan on the strength of the company they wanted to form, to be paid back as the money was earned.

Since they had enough money saved to put up a little over half of what they needed to start the store, they found that they were eligible for a regular business loan. It was a type of debt financing available to them locally.

Since Bob was not going to quit his job with the county and would have a steady income, he could cosign the loan. And since as librarian Jennifer had enough pertinent business experience to run the bookstore, she could qualify for a business loan herself. They would have to write up an application for such a loan.

HOW TO WRITE UP A LOAN APPLICATION

In a discussion with one of the bank officials, Jennifer and Bob learned what to include in their application for a business loan. Although such applications differ from place to place, they usually include the following key elements:

❑ *An opening statement.* This is a general opening state-ment about the amount of money you want and for what purpose you want to use it. In the case of Jennifer and Bob, that meant the amount of the loan and the name of the bookstore, which they had decided to call The Paper Tree.

❑ *The rationale for the loan.* This is a statement outlining exactly what kind of business you intend to open and how you hope to run it and why you think it will be successful. In this part of the application, you put as much hard sell as you can into your presentation.

❑ *A résumé, or résumés.* This part of the loan application resembles a typical job résumé, including the usual points covered in a business résumé:
    short bio
    education background
    job experience
    description of job experience
    experiences related to business

If two people are involved, as were Jennifer and Bob, each should include a separate résumé.

❏ *A personal statement.* The word "personal" here is misleading. Actually, a personal statement is really a financial statement of your own personal assets, your liabilities, your bank and insurance references, your sources of income, and your debts.

❏ *A one-year business projection.* This is an estimate of your gross sales for the first year you are going to be in business. It simply is a detailed account of what you intend to make, month by month. The projection should include turnover figures for every category of merchandise you plan to sell. If you are going to perform a service or produce a product, it should include the number of jobs and items involved, along with the revenue you hope to make from each.

❏ *A three-year business projection.* This is an earnings estimate for three years of business operation. This is an extension of the previous item, including detailed analyses of three years of operation of the business.

❏ *A month-by-month projection.* This monthly sales breakdown should contain detailed information of income and expenditures month by month for the first year. This is a more detailed and elaborate analysis than the previous ones, including liabilities and items of overhead.

Getting the Business Rolling

When Jennifer and Bob finally located an empty shop and were able to settle with the owner on the rent, the two of them then looked up suppliers of all the items they intended to sell. Finally they had the working figures to put into their loan application. Then they made up their proposal and took it to the bank.

They were stunned when the bank officials—people

they had known for years—told them that, all things considered, their proposal asked for too much money. Jennifer and Bob felt that they had made a fair estimate of their potential needs and had not been out of line in asking for $25,000 to start up their shop.

It was at that point Bob suggested to Jennifer they go bank shopping. There were other banks, he reminded her, although the two of them had always dealt with one. And so they visited various banks in the area, one by one, using the same proposal they had prepared for their own bank.

For anyone interested in getting a bank loan to start a business venture, it is good policy to shop around as a matter of course, even though you have one specific bank in mind to begin with. All banks are different—as different as the people who run them. Quite frequently a borrower may be able to get a much better deal at an unfamiliar bank than at the typical "friendly banker" already known.

It must be remembered that the entrepreneur/borrower is in the driver's seat when it comes to negotiating a loan. The borrower should never feel that it is the banking institution that controls the decisions. As long as the proposal is good, the entrepreneur has every reason to get the best possible financial arrangement available—no matter what it is.

Jennifer and Bob did find another bank, one that offered them more than their own bank would, and without any special strings attached. However, they did have to scale down their original request by several thousand dollars. In addition, they found that the interest for the loan would be taken off the top; of the $20,000 which was the amount finally decided on, $5,000 was interest and as interest was immediately deducted from the total. So Jennifer and Bob were in debt for $20,000, but only had the use of $15,000.

Working quickly, the two of them persuaded their suppliers to give them extended credit to make up the difference. Most of the suppliers agreed and the loan went through.

The shop did well enough to survive in its first years of operation. The main items, the books, sold slowly but steadily. The records and tape cassettes were an instant hit, but then their sales gradually tapered off. The furniture kits were a steady item. The only disappointment was the plants, which failed to do well even at Christmas time.

In the second year, Jennifer decided to cut back on the plants and use that part of the shop to sell toys, which went over big during the Christmas holidays and remained steady sellers throughout the year.

Most businesses, like that started by Jennifer and Bob, are begun with a combination of capital supplied by the owner and operator and someone else as well, such as a bank or lending institution, or a venture capital group—people in the business of putting up money for new projects.

Generally, the amount of money you can get from a bank or lending institution is usually less than the amount of money you have on hand to put into the company. It would be foolhardy to think that you could start a business with less than half the money in cash on hand.

The "borrower's packet" used by Jennifer and Bob is a typical rundown of the facts and figures that should be included in a business loan application. Let's take the points one by one and look at them a little more closely, seeing exactly how these points might be covered in a different type of proposed operation.

THE ANATOMY OF THE BORROWER'S PACKET

The Opening Statement

NAME: The Paper Tree

PRODUCTS: Books, Records, Furniture Kits, Plants

CAPITAL NEEDS:
Renovations, fixtures, equipment: $
Inventory: $
Owner investment: $

TOTAL: $

The Rationale for the Loan

After the opening statement, a typical section might include a number of reasons for opening up the business:

❑ There is no similar shop in the community.

❑ There is no similar shop in any of the surrounding communities or towns.

❑ The nearest competition is twenty miles away.

❑ Suppliers of books, records, and furniture kits will give discounts allowing the shop owner to be competitive with the nearest similar shop.

❑ The shop will offer local people the convenience of shopping for books and records.

❑ The money will remain in the community.

❑ The location is perfect for maximum exposure to traffic.

❑ The backgrounds of the proprietors have prepared them for running the shop.

❑ Each is aware of current reading trends.

❑ Each has the ability to deal with the public.

❑ Each has a knowledge of plants and furniture.

❑ Each has been living in the community for at least five years.

❑ The proprietors have outstanding credit ratings.

Every "rationale" for a loan application is going to be different, of course, but each follows an accepted pattern as above, stressing the pertinent details in each separate case.

The Résumé

The following section of the packet includes a résumé, or résumés, explaining succinctly the background of the proprietor or proprietors:

NAME: Jennifer Smith Johnson

ADDRESS: End Road, Land's End, Illinois.

BIO: Born and grew up in Land's End. Educated in Land's End Public Schools and the University of Chicago. Married and the mother of two children.

JOB EXPERIENCE: Assistant Librarian, Land's End Library, Illinois. Librarian, Land's End High School, Illinois.

DESCRIPTION OF EXPERIENCE:
During my ten years at the Land's End Library, I moved up from check-out assistant to acquisitions manager, and indexing specialist. I was in charge eventually of all the other library personnel, including check-out personnel and other members of the staff. Five years ago I was offered the job of head librarian at the high school, and was hired to upgrade and expand the school library, which had not managed to keep up with the high-tech changes in education. There I instituted a computer system to keep tabs on the books and worked out a borrowing system that reduced book-stealing. Although I have an excellent future with the school system, I feel it is time to resign in order to start my own bookstore and business.

Note that the résumé includes mention of the applicant's business skills and interests, stressing the accomplishments that demonstrate her business acumen. It is advisable for you to make every part of the loan application as hard-sell as possible, stressing your achievements and potential in any way you can whenever possible.

The Personal Statement

As has been said, the personal statement is really a financial statement of your personal finances, with figures usually filled out in a form supplied by the bank, lending institution, or venture capital group. The statement includes a detailed rundown of all assets and liabilities, annual sources of income, contingent liabilities, personal information, and general information about your finances.

It also includes mention of U.S. government and marketable securities, non-marketable securities, interest in real estate equities, real estate owned, life insurance carried, and names of banks or finance companies where credit has been obtained.

Under assets and liabilities, you should include the amount of cash on hand or in banks, along with real estate owned, personal property of value, securities, and so on. Under liabilities you should include notes payable to banks, both secured and unsecured, amounts payable to others, accounts and bills due, real estate mortgages payable, and so on.

Under sources of income, you should include your salary, bonuses and commissions of any kind, dividends, real estate income, and any other income.

Under personal information you should include number of children, dependents, and other details.

Under contingent liabilities you should include leases or contracts, legal claims, contested income, or cosigned loans.

As for general information, you should include pledged assets, legal actions against you, your bankruptcy history, if any, and other such information.

The One-Year Business Projection

In writing up a projection of the gross sales of the proposed business for a year, you should pay particular attention to your inventory and its cost, the market expected, and how much turnover you think you should have during the year. (Turnover means the actual purchase of an item and its sale. If you expect to sell every item three times a year, then your turnover is three times a year.)

If you plan to run a store selling books or toys, you would present your figures in this fashion:

BOOKS:
Inventory $
Plus 40 percent $
   TOTAL: $
Turnover: 3 times a year $
   TOTAL PROJECTION: $

TOYS:
Inventory $
Plus 35 percent $
   TOTAL: $
Turnover: 2 times a year $
   TOTAL PROJECTION: $

In the above breakdown, the inventory is the amount spent on the purchase of books before the shop even opens its doors. This will constitute the largest amount of your inventory in this type of business.

The 40 percent listed in the following line is the amount of your markup. That is the usual figure for a book markup, which is pretty well set by the list price on the dust jacket.

The "total" line is the total of the amount spent plus the 40 percent markup. This figure is included to show the amount you think you can gross from the inventory on hand.

The "turnover" line shows what you anticipate the regularity of sales to be for your stock. If you are correct and if you sell your inventory three times a year, then your total gross income will be three times the total in the line above.

Your total projection, then, will be three times the

amount of the original inventory plus markup. That shows what you expect to bring in in your first year.

You should make up a list of each type of merchandise you intend to sell.

The Three-Year Business Projection

This is a bit more complicated than the one-year projection. It should include all the following items, with the figures for each year listed in three separate columns: Year One, Year Two, and Year Three.

Here are the listings at the beginning of each line:

	Year One	Year Two	Year Three
GROSS SALES:	$	$	$
COST OF GOODS SOLD:	$	$	$
Inventory:	$	$	$
Purchases:	$	$	$
Goods Available:	$	$	$
End Inventory:	$	$	$
Cost of Goods Sold:	$	$	$
GROSS PROFIT:	$	$	$
OPERATING EXPENSES:	$	$	$
Rent:	$	$	$
Interest:	$	$	$
Utilities:	$	$	$
Insurance:	$	$	$
Supplies, office:	$	$	$
Transportation:	$	$	$
Dues:	$	$	$
Reference books:	$	$	$
Telephone:	$	$	$
Salaries:	$	$	$
Advertising:	$	$	$
Miscellaneous:	$	$	$
GROSS EXPENSES:	$	$	$
NET INCOME:	$	$	$

The Month-by-Month Business Projection

The final page of the loan application includes a monthly breakdown of the first year, with the percentage of sales projected for the year, the amount grossed on items sold, and the total.

In the end, the percentages should equal 100, with the categories adding up to the gross sales.

Outline for a Business Plan

You might want to obtain money a year or so after you open up a business. You can use the same type of statement already outlined, or you can draw up what is called a "business plan"—actually much the same thing as the loan application outlined above. The purpose is exactly the same: to obtain operating money.

Here is a suggested outline for such a plan. All you need do is fill it in in accordance with the details discussed above.

(1) COVER SHEET
   Name of business
   Names of principals
   Address and phone number of business

(2) STATEMENT OF PURPOSE

(3) THE BUSINESS
   Description
   Market
   Competition
   Location
   Management
   Personnel
   Application and expected effect of loan
   Summary

(4) FINANCIAL DATA
Sources and applications of funding
Capital equipment list
Balance sheet
Break-even analysis
Income projections
 i. Three-year summary (profit and loss)
 ii. Detail by month, first year
 iii. Detail by quarter, second year
 iv. Detail by quarter, third year
 v. Notes of explanation
Cash-flow projections
 i. Detail by month, first year
 ii. Detail by quarter, second year
 iii. Detail by quarter, third year
 iv. Notes of explanation
Deviation analysis
Financial reports
 i. Balance sheets, three years
 ii. Income statements, three years
 iii. Tax returns, three years

(5) SUPPORTING DOCUMENTS
Personal résumés
Personal financial requirements
Personal financial statements
Cost of living budget
Credit reports
Letters of reference
Job descriptions
Letters of intent
Copies of leases
Contracts
Legal documents
Anything else relevant to business plan

Where to Get Loans

If you are unable to get a bank loan at your local bank or lending institution, you can always ask the officials who turned you down why they refused it. Perhaps they will be able to give you some advice on changing the pitch of your application.

If you need help in preparing such an application, you can always try the Small Business Administration's Loan Guarantee Program. If your application proves too risky for your local bank, you can always send the application packet to the loan officers in your nearest S.B.A. office, with the request that they review it.

At least two loan officers read every application referred to the S.B.A. If one of the two officers thinks the application worthy of approval, your bank will be notified that the S.B.A. is in the position to underwrite the major part of your loan. The final loan will be granted through your bank, but the S.B.A. will act as guarantor of the loan, making the transaction smoother and easier for the bank.

You cannot apply directly to the S.B.A. for help in the Loan Guarantee Program. Your only access is through the loan department of a bank; you must of course be turned down by the bank to be granted access to the program.

Another Possibility: OMBE

You may be able to ask for help in getting a business loan at the Office of Minority Business Enterprise (OMBE), started in 1969 as part of the Department of Commerce in order "to increase minority business ownership to enable minority citizens to compete for their fair share of business sales and profits."

Although there are 35 million minority citizens in the country—17 percent of the population—only 4 percent of all businesses are owned by members of minorities, accounting for less than 1 percent of all business profits made.

6

Partnerships and Individual Proprietors

A CASE HISTORY

When Diana first considered opening up a word-processing business, she was shrewd enough to realize she would not be able to operate it all alone as an individual proprietor. Although she possessed all the skills needed to perform word-processing chores herself, she would not have any time left over to go out and acquire new business.

Such a situation, she decided, would be fatal. The business would soon reach a dead end. She knew her principal asset was an ability to generate and promote business; what she wanted was someone else to take care of the actual work at the word processor.

Her resolution of the problem was to seek out a partner who would complement her skills and establish a partnership.

A Partner for Diana

Her first choice was Elizabeth. Elizabeth was an accountant with a good knowledge of finances and bookkeeping—both abilities that would come in handy in helping run the business. Besides her skills, Elizabeth was a fast friend, someone with whom Diana had grown up and gone to school.

When approached, Elizabeth was agreeable to the arrangement. The two of them began looking around for office space, with Diana using her knowledge of the data processing market and her skills at organization to select the proper place to open up. She wanted her word-processing service to be located less than half a mile away from the large university in town, since most of her prospective clients were nearby. Diana at last found a place she liked and took Elizabeth there for her reaction.

Somehow the whole idea of opening up an office floored Elizabeth. As a prospective thing, largely imaginary, going into business was certainly a fine thing. But when it came down to the nitty-gritty, Elizabeth simply couldn't face it.

Diana was all set to sign a lease for the space with the owner of the building when she realized that Elizabeth was showing signs of nervousness and near collapse. To her dismay, Elizabeth backed out of the arrangement. Since the two of them had not signed any contract to legalize their partnership, there was no legal problem. Elizabeth simply went her own way, leaving Diana no recourse but to back out of the tentative agreement with the owner of the building.

Partner Number Two

Sadder but wiser, Diana decided that Elizabeth might be a good corporate person, but was simply not cut out to be an entrepreneur. Running a business was something quite different from serving as a cog in a corporate machine. It took different talents and different goals.

There was nothing for it but to seek another partner. And finally Diana thought she had found the proper complementary type of partner. This one was named Randy. He was a whiz-bang business graduate with excellent financial expertise. At least Diana would be able to leave the legalities and the commercial aspects of business to him; she would manage the office, acquire new clients, and get the work done. He even promised to put up money for the venture, something that Elizabeth had not been able to do.

Within months Diana was searching again for a place to open up. Randy, being a good businessman, drew up a contract of partnership between the two of them, including the amount of money each would put up to start the operation. It was all strictly business. Diana approved of his modus operandi.

Where's the Money?

The office opened several months after the partnership contracts were signed. The future looked rosy. There were some clouds on the horizon, but Diana hoped they might clear away. One cloud was Randy's failure to advance the money he had promised. Diana had to borrow money on her own to get the company started. In addition to that, Randy spent little time at the office; he seemed always out looking for business. Yet he didn't seem to be getting any.

Within months, Diana knew that the partnership was doomed. Randy wasn't as interested in the venture as he should be, nor was he able to attract enough new clients to keep the business growing. He seemed to be spending a great deal of his time on other projects that had nothing to do with Diana's word-processing company.

The Breakup of the Partnership

When she sat down with him several months later to try to work out some way to dissolve the partnership, she found to her surprise that Randy had no intention of letting go. He told her that in spite of what she thought, things were going very well. He had dozens of prospects who would soon be buying service.

But no such clients appeared. With the company's prospects withering because of the lack of new business, Diana faced Randy in a heated confrontation. When he finally realized that she did indeed mean to break up the partnership, he told her that he would go along—but only if she paid him a sum satisfactory to him to do so.

Diana was appalled. Not only was she unable to pay the amount he wanted, but she did not think she should have to pay him anything. He had reneged on his own written promise to put up money; he had failed to bring in enough clients to keep the business going.

After many months of battle—arguments and recriminations that were emotionally taxing on both participants—Randy finally withdrew, leaving Diana to continue the business alone.

For a while Diana found that she was doing very well as a sole proprietor. However, she soon realized she was much more interested in building up the business and getting new customers than she was in sitting down at the word processor and doing work for pay.

83

The 35 Percent Partner

Within a year, Diana met Constance, a married woman with a family who operated her own word-processing business. Diana contracted out some of her work to Constance, and in doing so found she was a good worker. The two of them got along well. In fact, Constance complemented Diana—she was low-pressure, cool, and calm. After a few months of profitable work together, Diana suggested that Constance become her partner on a 35–65 percent basis.

Constance agreed, and became a 35 percent partner. Her own company was merged into Diana's. Almost immediately, business picked up and the team began to make more money on a day-to-day basis than Diana had ever made before. Sales were tripling each month instead of doubling, as they had been when Diana was operating the company on her own.

Nevertheless, Constance, with her husband and family, was finding it too difficult to keep up with the increasing number of orders that Diana brought in. She found that her time with her family was being eroded. She was exhausted by the pressures that were on her during the workday. After nine months, she announced to Diana that she wanted out of the venture. It was taking too much of her time and energy and hurting her personal life.

Diana decided she would have to dissolve the partnership and continue on her own once again. By this time she was completely disillusioned with partnerships and business relationships of all kinds.

The End of the Search

"Elizabeth was a perfect company woman," Diana noted. "She would do well in the corporate hierarchy. But she was not a risk-taker. Randy was great at business—his own business. If he'd spent half as much time working for me as working to get money out of me, we'd have succeeded admirably! As for Constance, she's a hard worker and a perfect wife and mother, but she's not too great at putting energy into a business. People are just different."

Needless to say, Diana never again tried a partnership. Instead of that, she finally advertised for an office manager to handle the business details and eventually hired a woman who worked directly for her at regular compensation. Diana learned it was as hard to make a business partnership work as it was to make a marriage work.

Diana's experience is proved out in the business world generally.

The Law of Two Thirds

One recent survey showed that of 170 small businesses started by partners, more than two thirds of them broke up within a year or two. Over half of those breakups—60 percent—occurred because of the changing interests of the individuals involved, or because of personal conflicts.

In spite of Diana's unfortunate experience with partnerships, she was quite right in her original intention of experimenting with a partnership. In business, a team of two or more people with the proper complementary business skills can create a business with growth potential greater than a business created by an individual entrepre-

85

neur. Combinations of individuals, the old business maxim goes, are better than the sum of their parts.

That doesn't mean that a partnership is, per se, better than an individual proprietorship. To quote Gordon Baty, author of *Entrepreneurship for the Eighties:*

> If your analysis shows that you can do it alone, don't be afraid to try it. If you discover, as things progress, that you really *do* need a couple of partners, it's easier to get them later than it is doing it the other way around.

Three Ways to Set Up a Business

There are advantages as well as disadvantages in partnerships, as well as individual proprietorships. There are also advantages and disadvantages in incorporating oneself, and in creating a cooperative.

Actually, there are three basic ways to set up a business. All the rest of the methods are combinations of them:

❑ individual proprietorship

❑ partnership

❑ incorporation

A cooperative, for example, is a combination of a corporation and a partnership. And there are other notable combinations.

For now, let's take a closer look at the first two, individual proprietorship and partnership. We'll cover the corporation in the next chapter, along with the cooperative.

You should know something about the difference between operating a business as an individual, and operating it as a partnership. Most businesses, as a matter of fact, go through at least two types of organizational structure during their lives.

ANATOMY OF THE INDIVIDUAL PROPRIETORSHIP

The simplest form of business structure is the type that most people start out with. It is that favored by the entrepreneur—and for good reason.

The sole proprietorship is the one-owner business. It is the easiest kind of business to set up because it needs no special license from the government. However, the name of the business will probably have to be registered.

As a sole proprietor, you do not need a lawyer to set up the business. You do not need a lawyer to end it, either. You simply let the rest of the world know that you are in business—and that's it. If you decide to quit the business, you merely tell people you're not in business anymore.

If you are going to conduct a business under a name of some kind—The Paper Tree, The Green Door, or whatever—most states require that you register the name so they can find you if they need you. The registration form you use is known as a DBA—"Doing Business As"—available at your local county clerk's office, or at the state department of taxation.

In order to set up a business bank account, you will need a federal employer-identification number. All you have to do is give the bank your social security number or file Form SS-4, available from the IRS. That form states your name, your address, and information about your proposed business venture.

Advantages of an Individual Proprietorship

The biggest advantage of an individual proprietorship is that it allows you to run your own show, at your own pace, and as you alone see fit. Since there are no co-owners or partners to consult, you can make decisions and act on them immediately, and that can help make things run smoothly and profitably.

To start a business you do not necessarily need legal help, as I said before, but you should be legally competent to enter into a contract with another party. You must conduct your business in a manner that does not infringe upon or impede the legal rights of others.

In other words, you must be sure you are running your business in an area that is zoned for it; and you must have a license to run it if a license is required by local law.

The profits from your own business belong to you, but so do all the losses. You report them on your own personal income tax return.

Disadvantages to an Individual Proprietorship

The major disadvantage of being an individual proprietor is the fact that you become personally liable for all business debts, no matter how they are incurred. If a legal judgment is won against your business, you *personally* are in trouble—not just as a business entity. To pay off a legal judgment, the court can seize all your personal property. "All" means *all*—including all real estate, automobiles, and almost everything else you own.

One other disadvantage is the fact that you cannot procure capital to finance your business as easily as you could if you were incorporated, or if you were one of a number of partners. A bank tends to lend money to an incorporated business more readily than to an individual operator. In fact, a partner may become a partner simply to supply money to run a business.

In the long run, your main disadvantage is the fact that you will have a more limited outlook on the business than you would if you were working with someone else. You become boxed in by your own finite range of knowledge and know-how. If you are inexperienced, have not studied business at school, cannot improvise solutions to keep the business going, or if you try to respond quickly to business situations without knowing what to do, you are less likely to successfully operate a business as a sole owner, and more likely to make mistakes. With a partner, you may be able to operate much more efficiently because of the added dimension of expertise available to you.

ANATOMY OF THE PARTNERSHIP

A partnership consists of an organization involving two or more co-owners engaged in a legal business for the purpose of making a profit. A partnership can be set up in the same way an individual proprietorship is—simply by saying it exists. It can be ended in the same way. Or you can hire a lawyer to draw up a partnership agreement outlining the relationships of all partners and indicating how and when the partnership may be dissolved.

Some states require a partnership to file a certificate either in the county clerk's office or with the state, identifying each and every partner in the arrangement. If the partnership operates under a name of any kind, you must fill in a DBA form.

Different Types of Partnerships

There are a number of different types of partnerships. There is a general partnership, and a limited partnership, to name the two basic types. There is also the so-called ordinary partnership that can be either general or limited.

❏ *The ordinary partnership.* This type of partnership allows each member of the team to share equally in the profits made by the group, and in all the debts assumed by the group.

❑ *The general partnership.* This is a slight variation on the ordinary partnership. One member of the team is designated to run the business, with all the other partners in limited roles, acting as investors, with no other services required or rendered.

❑ *The limited partnership.* This is another variation on the ordinary partnership. In this type of partnership the partners are "limited," meaning that not only does each have a restricted role in the running of the partnership, but each has a limited liability up to the amount of money invested.

A partnership may designate unequal shares of profits to all partners. The number of shares a person is allocated usually depends on the amount of money he or she provides to start up the business in the first place. Roughly speaking, the partner putting up 25 percent of the money will receive 25 percent of the profits.

In a partnership, there is usually a legally binding contract setting forth the structure of the organization, with details of who each partner is, and the amount of his or her investment, their duties, and how each will share in the profits and losses.

The First Six Months Are the Hardest

A partnership serves a positive function beyond the monetary one. It can relieve the feeling of loneliness inherent in an individual proprietorship—especially in those crucial first days, weeks, and months. A partnership can also serve to sharpen the decision-making process, allowing the proprietors to dream up a greater choice of options than an individual owner might.

A partnership tends to be more successful than a sole proprietorship. A survey by *Inc* magazine of the year's one hundred fastest-growing companies found that two thirds were partnerships, and that within that group, three fourths were still in business at the time of the survey.

The co-owner of a successful store in the Northeast recently said:

> Going through the starting-up process together has been an important factor in helping solidify the partnership. The first six months were discouraging. We were able to give each other a lot of support during the tough times. Now business is picking up, and we're able to appreciate it together.

Advantages of a Partnership

The advantages of a partnership seems obvious. Two heads, they say, are always better than one. And, with two or more people working together, each is motivated to apply his or her best abilities by a direct sharing of the profits.

Besides that, it is much harder to stand on one leg than on two. As for three legs, a stool is more solid than a two-legged animal. Four legs give even more stability.

The key advantage to a partnership is the ability of one partner to complement—to complete, in a sense—the other. A two-dimensional approach to a problem is always better than one limited to a single point of view. Not everyone can be the genius who needs only one chance to solve a problem.

Disadvantages of a Partnership

Although two heads are better than one, and two legs better than one, two people may sometimes differ radically in their methods of solving a problem. A partnership can be as tricky as a marriage, as has already

91

been said. Personal problems may get in the way of doing business. Even psychological problems may crop up.

One important financial disadvantage in a partnership is the fact that legally a partner is not merely responsible for 25 percent of the debt if he has put up 25 percent of the start-up money, but is responsible for the full 100 percent of any business debt that has been assumed by the organization—except in a limited partnership.

There is another potential disadvantage in a situation in which one partner retires, quits, or dies. The remaining partner is left holding the bag.

In the case of hopeless and unresolvable differences between partners, the problem may arise as to who buys out whom. To prevent such a dispute, individuals becoming partners should write into their contract a way of resolving such a situation.

One should never forget the wise Frenchman's maxim about having an affair: it's ten times harder to break off an affair than begin it!

SOLE PROPRIETORSHIP OR PARTNERSHIP?

Should you opt for sole proprietorship or a partnership?

Actually, there is no way to answer this question without delving into the details of each individual situation. Even if you are a person who gets along with anybody, who likes people, and who feels you should have a partner in a business, you may simply not be able to find the right person at all.

On the other hand, if you are a loner, and want to work by yourself, you may find after a while that you would do better if you had a partner to help you steer your way around the shoals of business problems.

A successful business partnership is usually the result of the satisfaction of a number of tangible and intangible requirements at the same time.

One of these requirements is time together. Successful

partners usually start a business together and work hard during those early days. In that way, both partners manage to use their skills and ingenuity to work their way through immediate problems threatening the new venture; they learn to work as a team.

Another requirement is a combination of complementary personalities. Everyone is different from everyone else. If you are aggressive, you may find that a partner who is not aggressive may balance you effectively. If you are a doer, your partner might well be a visualizer or a talker—that is, a salesperson.

Making the Most of Skills

Still another requirement is the possession of skills that balance one another. You should possess skills that your partner does not possess; and he or she should possess skills that you do not. Partners should extend beyond one another in different directions.

If you're a mechanic who knows cars, don't get together with another mechanic who knows cars to start up a repair business. Even if you're going to run a garage, get a salesperson, or a person with different skills from yours. If you're both skilled at exactly the same thing, you'll be quarreling with each other or competing with each other to the detriment of the job you're trying to do together. Or you may think and respond exactly alike, thus missing out on ways to solve problems.

On the other hand, your sense of values—your way of looking at life—should be similar. If one partner wants to work all the time and the other wants just to work nine to five, it simply isn't going to work.

As you can see, partnership in business is almost as complex as partnership in marriage. It takes a lot of luck—and hard work—to get either one to work right.

7

Corporations and Cooperatives

A CASE HISTORY

Allen and Marcus were two practicing veterinarians who graduated from school at about the same time and decided to open up a practice together. They formed a partnership and began to serve a suburban community in the Midwest. From the beginning their partnership was very successful.

Except for one thing: the partnership was hit by a malpractice suit in the early years. The situation was extremely precarious at one point, because both Allen and Marcus had to take out second mortgages on their homes in order to pay for legal help in fighting the suit.

The High Cost of Incorporation

During this rather frustrating and frightening episode, the two veterinarians began looking at their business situation in a different light. They had considered incorporating their business from the beginning, but had opted against it because of the cost involved in incorporation. They would have to pay city corporation tax, state corporation tax, as well as corporate income tax (which taxes twice). And the rates were very high.

Nevertheless, with the lawsuit staring them in the face, and the possibility that a judgment against them could deprive them of all their personal assets as well as their business, they decided that if they were fortunate enough to get out of the situation they were in, they would incorporate. It would save them from being personally responsible for every move they made.

Luckily they did win the lawsuit, and continued in business. And they did eventually turn their partnership into a corporation. And in spite of the added costs—the FICA tax for a corporation was 13.7 percent—they were more easy in their minds about any malpractice suit that might be filed against them.

Working as a Corporation

In turn, they were able to deduct their health, life, and disability insurance coverage; as a partnership, they had not been able to do so. They were also able to set aside larger retirement amounts, larger than they were allowed as business partners. And so they continued work for some years as a corporation.

Then in 1982, the situation changed once again. The Tax Equity and Fiscal Responsibility Act of 1982 took away one of the primary benefits of incorporation: Allen and Marcus were no longer allowed to put aside their large retirement allocations. A new limit was set at $30,000 or 25 percent of earned income, whichever was less.

Nevertheless, Allen and Marcus continued to operate as a corporation, in spite of the temptation to return to partnership status. In their business, with its constant risk of malpractice suits and other types of liability, they felt they were better off acting as a corporation than as partners.

Let's take a closer look at this third type of business organization—the corporation.

ANATOMY OF A CORPORATION

A corporation is a legal creation—a kind of android acting as a business. The corporation (the word comes from the Latin *corpus* = body) can be owned by you as an individual, or by you in partnership with a number of other people. In the latter case, each person buys into the "body" through shares in the corporation's capital stock.

It is the corporation that does the hiring, firing, and buying and selling, all in accordance with the laws of the state where it is incorporated. A corporation is set up by what is called a "charter." It is probably best to become incorporated through legal channels by a lawyer. The fees range anywhere from $250 to $400.

All assets of the corporation are owned by the corporation—not by the shareholders.

Advantages of Incorporation

The most important advantage in the creation of a corporation is that it limits your liability to a fixed amount, usually the amount of your investment in the corporation. Therefore, if the corporation becomes liable for a large sum of money, your own personal property is protected from seizure by the courts.

Another important advantage of a corporation is the relative ease with which it can secure capital in large amounts from many different sources. It's much easier to receive financial help for a corporation than for an individual proprietor or for a partnership.

Another advantage is that an individual proprietor must pay for his hospitalization insurance right out of his own pocket. In a corporation, such an expense can be handled in the overall management and running of the company.

Disadvantages of Incorporation

One of the main disadvantages of creating a corporation is the cost. In addition to that, a corporation pays taxes on its profits at a different rate than an individual. These higher rates tax the corporation's net income—income after paying out all the salaries of the officers in the company.

Since the corporation pays its own income tax on its net profit, and then distributes the remainder of the net to its shareholders, all shareholders will pay a *second* personal income tax on the money made in profit.

Another problem with a corporation is that there are extensive government regulations and burdensome local, state, and federal reports that must be filed.

For example, in New York State, there is a franchise tax for corporations. And in New York City, there is also an income tax on corporations. Add to that the bookkeeping and the clerical costs, and you're out a lot of money.

In a corporation, you cannot keep social security taxes low. A corporation pays FICA (Social Security) taxes at the rate of 13.7 percent. A self-employed individual pays only a self-employment tax of 11.3 percent but, in a sole proprietorship or partnership, health, life, and disability insurance coverage for the principals in the business are *not* deductible.

Nevertheless, as explained in the case history at the head of the chapter, there have been recent changes in

97

the statutes that make operation as a corporation less advantageous than in previous years. The Tax Equity and Fiscal Responsibility Act of 1982 (TEFRA) wiped out one of the main benefits of incorporation—that of being able to set aside an amount of money for retirement larger than that allowed a sole proprietor or members of a partnership.

NOTE: Legislation concerning incorporation, sole proprietorship, and taxes at all government levels is subject to reform and change. It is essential that you keep up-to-date at all times with all statutes and regulations that might affect your enterprise in any of its details.

The Problems with TEFRA

One tax partner in a national accounting firm says flatly:

> Now the tax reasons for incorporating are not as material as they used to be.

TEFRA did not take away *all* advantages. You can still deduct the costs of medical, life, and disability insurance for principals in the company. And the company can also retain some of the profits. On that point, one accountant advises:

> Leave some earnings behind in the corporation. The first $100,000 of corporate income is taxed at an effective rate of only 26 percent. If you took out that extra $100,000, you'd be paying an individual income tax on it of 50 percent.

However, if you accumulate over $150,000 in earnings, you have to explain to the IRS why you did so. Also, by leaving too much money in the corporation, you may be subject to an accumulated earnings penalty. This penalty is 27.5 percent of the first $100,000 of taxable income that is unreasonably accumulated, and 38.5 percent on amounts in excess of $100,000—and that's in addition to normal income taxes!

Should You or Shouldn't You?

There's a general rule of thumb about whether or not to incorporate. One Boston tax executive boils it down to this:

If you don't need that protection—don't.

And he explains it this way:

> If you're a small retailer, you probably don't need to be incorporated. But if you're an insulation manufacturer with product liability, it makes sense to incorporate.

There is one special type of corporation that can **serve** as an option to the ordinary corporation just discussed. It is called the S Corporation—meaning "Subchapter Corporation." It is also known as the "pseudo" corporation.

Let's take a look at that for a moment.

ANATOMY OF THE S CORPORATION

The S corporation was set up by the IRS to help people involved in small-business management but having difficulty coping with the complications of running a typical corporation.

You get the same protection as an individual in a regular corporation—that is, you are not liable on a personal basis for debts incurred by the corporation—but your income is not subject to the corporate tax.

To qualify for S corporation status, your company must meet a number of requirements:

(1) It must be a domestic corporation. That is, it must be organized either in the United States or under federal or

99

state law. "Corporation" means joint-stock corporation, insurance corporation, or an association that has the characteristics of a corporation.

(2) It must not be a member of an affiliated group of corporations. It must not have a subsidiary. (It is a member of an affiliated group if it directly owns 80 percent or more of voting power in all classes of stock and 80 percent or more of each class of nonvoting common stock of another corporation.)

(3) It must have only one class of stock; that is, the dividend rights and liquidation preference for each share must be equal.

(4) It must not have more than thirty-five shareholders.

(5) It must have only individuals and their estates as shareholders. Partnerships and corporations cannot be shareholders.

(6) It must not have a nonresident alien as a shareholder. Anyone who is a shareholder must be a citizen or resident of the United States.

(7) It must not be any of the following:

- ❑ a domestic-based international sales corporation;
- ❑ a corporation that takes the tax credit for doing business in a United States possession;
- ❑ a financial institution that takes deposits and makes loans; or
- ❑ an insurance company taxed under international laws of the Internal Revenue Service.

If you fulfill all the requirements listed above, you and your corporation are eligible to file for S corporation status.

The S Corporation Tax Structure

In the S corporation, the tax structure resembles that of an ordinary partnership. Each shareholder must report his or her pro rata share of corporate profits as part of personal income, or deduct corporate losses from personal income (within certain limitations).

An S corporation offers the same protection as a regular corporation, as has been stated. You are not subject to corporate tax; instead, income flows through your personal tax return, just as it would if you operated your business as a sole proprietorship or partnership.

The choice between sole proprietorship or S corporation status must be made on the basis of whether it is still an advantage to incorporate, given the fact that you won't be able to retain some of the company earnings.

Running the S corporation can be a tricky business. The IRS does not allow you to switch back and forth from S corporation to individual proprietorship in accordance with your immediate needs. Also, the structuring of the S corporation must be scrupulously legal. It is essential that you have a lawyer to help you out.

Advantages of S Incorporation

Yet the advantages seem obvious:

❑ You avoid paying the regular corporate tax.

❑ The corporate long-term capital gains—after payment of capital gains tax—are taxed directly to the shareholders as a capital gain.

❑ The tax on unreasonable accumulations of earnings generally does not apply.

101

❏ You have the ability to remove previously taxed earnings from the corporation in cash without incurring the current dividends tax.

Disadvantages of S Incorporation

Nevertheless, there are disadvantages, as well as advantages:

❏ An S corporation is not allowed more than thirty-five shareholders. Even counting shareholders can be complicated too. For example:

(1) If stock is actually held by a trust, you must count the people who are considered to be shareholders. You do *not* count the trust itself as a shareholder.

(2) You count a husband and a wife and their estate or estates as one shareholder, even if they own stock separately.

(3) You count everyone who owns any stock, even if the stock is owned jointly with someone else.

❏ The receipt of too much passive income, or foreign income, may disallow S corporation status.

❏ Foreign tax credit is not allowed for foreign taxes paid by the corporation.

❏ The constructive dividend is considered received at the end of the corporation's tax year by people who are shareholders at the time.

And there are some other problems that might come up in the case of the S corporation:

❏ If you are refused S corporation tax status, you lose the right to nondividend treatment for previously taxed income.

❑ You are not allowed to pass on nondividend treatment for previously taxed income to another person.

❑ You cannot pass on nondividend treatment for cash contributions made within two and a half months after the close of the year elected to another person.

❑ Any net operating loss in excess of the adjusted basis of a shareholder's stock and indebtedness of the corporation to the shareholder is not deductible.

❑ Accrued compensation owed to related taxpayers not paid within two and a half months after the close of the tax year is treated as distribution of accumulated earnings and profits.

❑ Dividends received by members of a family group may be allocated to reflect value of services rendered.

❑ Recapture of investment credit is applicable to a year prior to the first year you choose to hold S corporation status, but it can be avoided by the shareholders' agreement to assume liability for the recapture of the tax.

❑ Transfer of stock in an S corporation to a corporation, a partnership, an ineligible trust, or a nonresident alien will disqualify an S corporation.

❑ Acquisition of a subsidiary other than certain types of nonoperative subsidiaries will disqualify an S corporation.

As you can see, there are complicated details involved in the S corporation. You should consult a tax authority before committing your business to this type of organization. However, there are advantages, which you should consider before you settle on any specific type of setup for your business.

There is yet another type of spin-off possible—the cooperative. The cooperative is a combination of partnership and corporation. This type of organization has come down to us through the years from the farming community, through urban housing, and through certain types of business organizations.

Let's take a look at the typical cooperative.

ANATOMY OF THE COOPERATIVE

A cooperative is usually created by a group of people who have a common economic or special physical need.

For example, a marketing cooperative may be set up by a group of designers and artisans who produce items they hope to sell. The cooperative handles the matter of marketing and retailing in the manner of a corporate business. The group may or may not be legally incorporated.

In some states, there are laws covering the cooperative. For example, the cooperative can become a corporation. In that case, the liability protection guards the members the same way a corporation's protection does. In addition, the cooperative pays taxes on profits through the corporation.

The Unincorporated Cooperative

When a cooperative is not incorporated, it is considered legally as a partnership with extended liabilities for all members. Profits in this instance are taxed as individual income.

The purpose of a retail-marketing cooperative is to display and sell merchandise more efficiently and more directly to achieve higher profits—cutting down an overhead and other out-of-pocket expenses.

When extra money accrues in a cooperative, it comes back to the members through refunds in proportion to the activity of each individual member. For example, a refund system might be set up to reflect the number of sales of each individual member's work; those selling the most will get back a larger proportion of the refund than those selling less. A refund, incidentally, is taxable as personal income. Thus from a tax standpoint a refund is essentially income profit.

Management of the Cooperative

A cooperative is usually managed by a board of directors and a hired manager, or by a management staff. The board or the staff is elected or hired by the cooperative itself.

When a member joins a cooperative he or she usually purchases shares of stock in the cooperative. No matter how many shares a new member buys, he or she only controls one vote. It is the members who elect the board of directors to oversee the day-to-day operation of the organization.

The success of a cooperative venture almost always depends on the ability and experience of whoever runs it— be it a manager, a group of executives, or an experienced cooperative head.

When a cooperative is disbanded, the assets and liabilities are distributed equally among all members.

How a Cooperative Differs from Other Forms of Business

A cooperative differs from all other types of business organizations in three basic areas:

(1) Allocation of profits.

(2) Allocation of control.

(3) Allocation of returns.

Allocation of Profits

The cooperative does not exist to make money for itself, in the manner of a corporation, a partnership, or an individual proprietorship. Rather, it exists in order to provide net margins of profits above the cost of providing the services.

In effect, all services in a cooperative are strictly *at cost.*

Any money earned above the amount put in belongs to the members of the cooperative, just as in a corporation, but the proportion of the profits are allocated not on the basis of a percentage of investment, but on a number of other criteria established by the governing body:

❑ patronage

❑ resource contribution

❑ labor

❑ any other predetermined factor

Allocation of Control

A cooperative is controlled on a basis other than the amount of capital contributed, as would be the case in a corporation or partnership. Generally, the basis for control is democratic: one member, one vote.

Because the cooperative is essentially a nonprofit organization, its control can be allocated in a more egalitarian manner than that of a partnership or corporation.

Thus the person or company in a cooperative who may provide more patronage, labor, and/or capital will still share equally in its control with every other member.

Allocation of Returns

As for allocation of returns, in a cooperative the return on investment is not based on the specific amount of capital ventured by any member. It is based on a formula determined by the various criteria established in setting up the cooperative. Thus the return on investment may vary in each individual case.

Advantages and Disadvantages of Cooperatives

The primary raison d'être of the cooperative—not to make a profit but to help out its members in some particular endeavor—is a disadvantage in itself to the person who has entrepreneurial instincts and wants to run a business successfully and make a profit.

And yet for the skilled artisan or specialist in a certain kind of service, the cooperative may be the answer when the product or the service does not fit into the general pattern of marketing techniques. For the individual who is not skilled at—or does not want to be skilled at—negotiating individual contracts and manipulating money, the cooperative is an excellent support system to make use of.

HOW TO CHOOSE A SPECIFIC BUSINESS STRUCTURE

It is of course advisable for anyone interested in entrepreneurship to weigh the different characteristics of these business enterprises in order to determine which direction is best to take.

Objectives differ in all these types of business structures. The individual proprietor is in business to profit for himself or herself. In a partnership, the purpose is to make a profit for the partners, who split it according to a prior agreement.

In a corporation, the profit over and above the operating expenses goes to the people who invest in shares of the enterprise (except in the case of an individual who incorporates himself or herself).

In a cooperative, the profit goes to the members and patrons according to a complex prearranged allocation—but one based strictly on egalitarian democratic principles.

Functions and Controls

The control differs in every one of these various types of enterprises.

For example, the individual proprietor exerts total control over the business he or she runs.

In a partnership, the partners exert control between or among themselves.

In a corporation, the investors exert control from outside—or from inside—according to a group selected to exert control.

In a cooperative, the members exert control, but in a one-member, one-vote manner.

The function does not differ in these various types of enterprises.

In a sole proprietorship, in a partnership, in a corporation, and in a cooperative, the function of the enterprise is the same:

❑ to buy or produce goods for sale, or to provide a service to the public

❑ to profit from the purchase, production, and marketing of goods and/or services to the public.

Legalities and Liabilities

The legal status of the four types of business also differs.

An individual may be unincorporated, or may be incorporated. In either case, he or she manages himself or herself without a legal agreement.

In a partnership, the partners become the managers. There is usually a legal agreement between the participants before the operation begins. These agreements are in accordance with the laws of the state or community.

A corporation is an organization incorporated under a particular state law. It is managed by a board of directors, selected by the members of the corporation in accordance with the original covenant of the corporation.

Depending on local law, a cooperative may be set up to resemble a partnership (unincorporated) or to resemble a corporation (incorporated). The cooperative is usually operated by a hired manager, who is in turn selected by a board of directors elected by the members of the cooperative.

As for liability:

The individual entrepreneur is responsible for all liabilities to the extent of both his business assets and his personal assets.

The partnership is liable for all liabilities to the total extent of all assets of all members of the partnership.

The corporation is liable to the extent of the assets of the corporation itself—and that is the full extent of the liability.

The cooperative is liable for the assets of the cooperative and to the extent of the cooperative only.

The Net Proceeds

As for who gets the net proceeds:

The individual proprietor gets all the profits.

The partnership gets the profits and divides them among the members of the partnership according to a prearranged plan.

The corporation divides the profits among the stockholders on the basis of each shareholder's original investment.

The cooperative divides the profits in proportion to the cooperative's special prearranged allocation, usually on a one-man, one-vote basis.

8

The Joys of Marketing

A TRUE STORY: I

Around the turn of the century, a young bank clerk named William Sydney Porter was imprisoned for embezzling bank funds. Porter was a personable young man who had what was then called the gift of gab. In his jail cell, he entertained his companions in misery with stories of people he had known on the outside. When he failed to recall the details of an incident he was relating, he made them up.

Because the hours in confinement hung heavily on him, he began to write down his tales during the evenings. It was this practice perfected in prison that gave Porter an opportunity to turn his talent into a commercial success when he was finally released.

Adopting the pseudonym O. Henry—probably so that no one would know that the story was written by an ex-con—Porter got a job on a New York newspaper where he continued to turn out his stories for magazines and newspapers both.

111

Birth of the Cisco Kid

He became one of the most popular and prolific short story writers of the era, at times compared to Mark Twain, an earlier American humorist who had also worked under a pseudonym. Although O. Henry's works have lost some of their glamour through the years, he did invent a handful of characters that still live in motion pictures and television—among them Jimmy Valentine (the ex-safecracker) and the Cisco Kid (the famed Western good-guy outlaw).

The point of this story is to show how a man with the gift of gab, a wild imagination, and time on his hands managed to parlay his talent into a commercial success—into a business of his own, really—by successfully knowing how to *market his product.*

Basically, all successful marketing entails the creation of some kind of supply to fulfill some kind of demand. Since everyone likes to hear or read a good story, Porter managed to fill that demand by writing down his stories for public consumption.

Not only was Porter able to successfully market his own talents, but he understood marketing in general, and knew that it was one of the most fascinating subjects to write about at that time. Americans in particular were excited about marketing.

One of his stories is a memorable example of one man's special marketing ingenuity.

A MADE-UP STORY

In this O. Henry story, the hero, a down-and-out salesman who had been driven out of his territory by bad blood between him and his supervisor, found himself dead broke in a small village far from the beaten path in the wilds of Central America. When he took a look around he realized that the villagers needed his help to bring them into the twentieth century.

As a former shoe salesman, he saw immediately that the villagers were in dire need—they walked around barefoot. Not one of them owned a pair of shoes. He realized he had been sent there by fate to help these people. All he had to do was send out for a supply of shoes, open up a shop, and put shoes on every villager within miles of the tiny town.

Eskimos, Refrigerators, Etc.

He finally managed to get in a large supply of shoes and open up a store. The problem was that even though the natives were interested in shoes as a curiosity, none of them really *needed* them, nor was one of them even remotely interested in trying them out.

Eventually the salesman managed to get one villager to put on a pair, but the shoes made his feet hurt. The news spread. No one in the village wanted shoes. The townspeople opted—to a person—to remain barefoot. No matter how hard the salesman tried to show them the fantastic advantages of shoes, no one would buy.

The Birth of an Idea

By now the salesman was in desperate financial straits. He owed money for the big shipment of shoes, and he had no prospects of selling any. He was roaming the countryside in desperation, trying to decide whether to flee on foot or vanish in some spectacular manner when he saw a runaway burro rush past him.

He followed the burro down into a ravine, finally tethered the beast to a bush, and waited for its owner to show up. When the owner arrived and thanked the salesman, he took off the burro's blanket under the pack saddle and examined the animal. A small burr had gotten wedged between the blanket and the hide of the animal. It was the pressure of the load on the hide that had caused the burro to bolt.

Thoughtfully the salesman strolled back to his over-stocked shop. That night he posted a letter to a friend in the United States. Soon another shipment arrived for him. The natives laughed at him, wondering what the containers held. Whatever it was, they were sure they would have no need for it—no more need than an Eskimo would have for a refrigerator.

Creating the Right Demand: I

The next day there was little laughter in the village. Instead, there were screams of agony and pain. One by one the villagers sheepishly limped into the salesman's shoe shop to purchase shoes. By the time evening had rolled around, he had sold out his supply and was taking orders for more.

The salesman had practiced one of the most time-honored and important elements of marketing: he had created a demand for a product. Never mind that he had done it in a devious manner. He already had the supply of shoes; he had a good product. But when he tried to sell the shoes to a population that was accustomed to going about barefoot he had forgotten that he did not have a proper demand for the product.

It was the shipment from the friend in the United States that had given him the golden opportunity during the night to create an instantaneous demand for shoes. And the cockleburrs in the shipment were much cheaper than the shipment of shoes!

Although the story told by the famed short story writer is a bit fanciful, it does illustrate an important point about marketing.

In real life, another turn-of-the-century entrepreneur did create a demand that had not previously existed for a product that had been around for a while.

A TRUE STORY: II

William Wrigley came upon a product that was in no way similar to the shoe salesman's time-tested and proven article of clothing. Wrigley's product was chicle, something from nature no one had any use for. The early American Indians had chewed spruce resin before the arrival of the white man, and the Yankees in New England took it up in early Colonial days. They used it as a kind of poor substitute for chewing tobacco.

In South America the natives chewed chicle, a natural product that was similar to spruce resin. Two Americans named William and Semple produced a chewing compound out of raw chicle and patented it, calling it "chewing gum." When Wrigley was a salesman peddling soap and baking powder from door to door, he used a chewing gum called Zeno as a giveaway to anyone who purchased his wares. Kids liked to chew it, pretending they were chawing tobacco; housewives often joined them.

The problem was that Zeno was drab and bland, and didn't stimulate the taste buds. It wasn't really good enough to be anything *except* a giveaway. But the idea of chewing gum as a product intrigued Wrigley and he moved to Chicago and bought into the company. At the time chicle was flavored with sugar and random spices to give it some bounce. Wrigley experimented with oils, mints, licorice, and fruit flavors, and finally came up with an improvement on any known gum. He called the flavor Juicy Fruit, and in 1891 produced the first Wrigley-flavored stick of chewing gum.

But how to sell it?

Chewing tobacco was popular with men, but messy, and disdained by women who preferred keeping spittoons out of the house and in the saloon. The idea

Wrigley had was to make chewing more socially accept-
able by substituting chicle for tobacco. To popularize his
idea, he advertised everywhere, packaged his gum in flat
sticks wrapped in bright colors, and talked up chewing as
a "national pastime."

He added flavor after flavor: Spearmint (named from
the regular mint leaf), Doublemint (Wrigley's ingenious
play on words to imply twice the taste), and others. He
even bought the Chicago Cubs baseball team, and soon all
the players were substituting Wrigley's gum for their tobacco chaws. Eventually secretaries all over the country
were chewing gum, too. Kids? Of course! Next to baseball, chewing gum *was* the national pastime.

Creating the Right Demand: II

Wrigley's methods were similar to the methods of O.
Henry's shoe salesman, and, in their own way, they were
as remarkable and as imaginative. Like the shoe salesman, Wrigley had to invent a desire and demand for a
product that was of no earthly use whatsoever, but was
simply an idea in the back of the head of a would-be mer-
chant.

But there was no easy, overnight, magical way to induce the public to demand chewing gum the way O.
Henry's salesman forced a demand for shoes on the cock-
leburr-infested village. Wrigley had to set about his education process in a painstaking, expensive, and artful
way—advertising it, promoting it, and pushing the little-
known product.

Desire for chewing gum was one of those things that he
had to build from the ground up, psychological brick by
psychological brick. But Wrigley was a meticulous man,
and within a few years he was able to create a desire in
the American people for a thing no one really wanted but
which soon became an obsession with millions.

He created the desire by heavy saturation advertising
in newspapers, magazines, and especially in the color

116

comics so popular with young people during the 1920s and 1930s. He created the desire by letting it be known that his substitute for tobacco was harmless, clean, and more civilized than tobacco. He created the desire by persuading baseball players—American heroes—to chew gum rather than tobacco.

His son, P. K. Wrigley, once described gum as an "adult pacifier," thus pointing up one of its subliminal qualities: chewing calmed the nerves.

During World War II, the company produced 600 million sticks of gum a month—and it all went into the mouths of members of the armed forces! Civilians simply didn't have any gum for the duration. By the war's end, P. K. Wrigley (William had died in 1932) was worth $100 million, an empire stuck together with chewing gum.

What *was* chewing gum, really?

Nothing. A giveaway gimmick that intrigued a man of imagination. Just an idea in the brain of a man with marketing sense, promotional instincts, and vision.

All three of the protagonists of these case histories were entrepreneurs in a very real sense. Almost any writer—poet, short story writer, novelist—has to have entrepreneurial instincts in order to succeed. There is a ' loneliness and an independence necessary for any person in the creative arts, whether he or she be writer, painter, or musician.

The Quintessential Entrepreneur

Almost any salesperson has to have some kind of business sense to sell something to a customer. Whether it is ingratiating charm, a psychological understanding of what makes people tick, or simply a talent for manipulating people to do something against their better judgment— the salesperson is the quintessential entrepreneur.

Almost any inventor or developer of a fad is an entrepreneur, too. American history is full of inventors—Benjamin Franklin, Eli Whitney, Robert Fulton, and all the rest who came up to push the Industrial Revolution into high gear during the eighteenth and nineteenth centuries. The high-tech operators of today are simply updated versions of the early inventors.

Let's take a look at exactly what the word "marketing" means and how it is applied to the business world today in relation to an individual entrepreneur. It is the secret of such a person's success or failure.

The word comes from the Latin, *mercatus,* meaning both "trade" and "marketplace." Today it means, specifically:

> the act or process of selling or purchasing in a market; or the aggregate of functions involved in moving goods from producer to consumer.

The Three Essentials of Marketing

For the entrepreneur or individual proprietor of a small business, effective marketing procedures may be difficult if not impossible to institute. In a large company, there is usually a special department that is concerned solely with marketing problems.

These are three basic marketing problems:

❑ obtaining correct marketing information

❑ analyzing marketing input

❑ interpreting overall marketing conditions

A small company cannot afford to staff a trained, professional research team or even hire a consultant to perform complicated studies. This means that most emerging companies must rely on the work of untrained people learning the intricacies of the operation from scratch to collect and analyze important marketing information.

This poses a major problem. Before going into the details of that problem and its many concomitants, let's take a look at the typical marketing questions that arise in a small-business venture—in *any* business venture, for that matter.

A LAUNDRY LIST OF MARKETING QUESTIONS

- ❑ Why do customers buy a particular product or service?
- ❑ Why does a customer choose a particular brand over another brand?
- ❑ Who buys the product or service provided by the entrepreneur?
- ❑ Who buys products or services from a competitor and why?
- ❑ Where is the decision made to buy a product or service?
- ❑ Where does a customer seek information about a product or service?
- ❑ Where do customers ordinarily purchase the product or service?
- ❑ When does a customer first make the initial decision to buy?
- ❑ When is the product or service purchased *again* by the customer?
- ❑ What are the psychological reasons that make a customer buy?
- ❑ How many times does the average customer buy a product or service?
- ❑ How long does the buying process last between seller and purchaser?
- ❑ Do all buyers actually use the product or service in question?

❏ How important is the consideration of life-style in the purchase?

❏ How much money is the customer willing to spend?

❏ What services is the customer being led to expect from the purchase?

❏ What are the most important buying criteria to the customer?

❏ How does the customer compare products and services with other similar products and services?

❏ What risks does the buyer perceive in a specific purchase?

❏ What is the potential of the entire market in relation to one product or service?

❏ Does the customer seek any particular benefits from the product or service?

❏ What factors influence the demand for the product or service?

❏ What important functions do the product or service perform for the buyer?

Answering These Important Questions

Every one of these questions is important in the overall marketing situation for any company—from a company run by an individual proprietor all the way up to an international super-conglomerate. At one time, each of these questions will become an important element in marketing that must be faced by any proprietor.

As to how to get these questions answered accurately, that is another problem. The question is, can a small firm conduct a meaningful marketing research program to find out if its product or service will sell well—or, indeed, sell at all?

The answer is that an individual proprietor can do so, provided he or she understands the problems involved and recognizes that research information is really an investment on which a return can be anticipated.

Initiating a Market Research Program

Briefly, here are the essential steps you should take to start up your own research program—either to be done by yourself, or to be assigned to a professional organization or consultant:

(1) Define the objective.

(2) Plan the research project.

(3) Gather the information.

(4) Test the market.

(5) Follow up the research.

Let's take a look at these steps one by one in a more detailed manner.

(1) DEFINING THE OBJECTIVE

The first step to take is to decide what project you want to take on. You may want to introduce a new product or a different kind of service. You may want to look into the possibility of establishing a new outlet for a business in another area. Or you may want to explore the idea of opening up a new territory to expand your current sales program.

Whatever your objective is, it must be clearly identified before you begin to take action of any kind. Although the establishment of a final goal is always a must in any plan of action, it is surprising how many would-be entrepreneurs fail to keep that objective in mind when they begin to take the plunge into the icy waters of commerce.

It is also surprising how many intelligent and imaginative people *think* they have specific marketing goals in mind when actually they don't have the haziest idea of what they are doing and don't have *anything* crisply delineated.

As a kind of test, answer the following questions about your own product or service and the kind of marketing survey you'd like to do. Then determine whether you have really managed to define the proper objective.

Check List for Defining Objectives

(1) What consumers do you think will use your product or service?

(2) What are the ages, locations, occupations, and income of your potential customers?

(3) Are you familiar with the competition and its good points and bad points?

(4) Have you searched out and identified all the possible competition?

(5) Do you think your price will compare favorably with the competition?

(6) What is the general market consumption of a product or service of this type?

(7) Does it seem as if the market will expand or decline in the next ten years?

(8) Have you explored all the possible selling techniques you should use?

(9) Have you settled on specific selling techniques to put to use?

(10) How will your customers pay—with cash, by company charge, by general credit card?

(11) If applicable, what is the peak season for the market you are operating in?

(12) Have you isolated the actual, specific marketing problem you are trying to solve?

(13) What do you really expect the results of the market research study to tell you?

(14) How accurate do you expect the information you get will be?

(15) Will there be any serious consequences if you make a wrong decision?

(16) Do you have an alternate course of action open to you in case of trouble?

(17) Are you familiar with the basic assumptions that are being made in the study?

(18) Are there any assumptions over which you have no control in making your study?

(19) What is already known about the subject under investigation?

(20) Is there any practical way you can check up on the accuracy of the information?

A thoughtful perusal of your answers to the above questions may show you that you have not really thought through your marketing survey. If you find that you haven't, it's time to get down to work right away and do so.

Then, when you've explored the matter for some time, you should put all these goals down in writing. It's best to start with the overall objective, stating it in one or two sentences. Then you can narrow these down into a list of specific information goals such as those mentioned above.

(2) PLANNING THE RESEARCH PROJECT

Once you have the objectives clearly in mind, then you can make a decision as to the kind of survey you should make in order to get the information necessary for your conclusions. In turn, you can then decide the approach to use to test the market.

Gathering marketing data is usually accomplished by asking questions and getting answers. In other words, research in this case is a kind of dialogue between you and the potential consumer (direct or indirect).

Because the project is basically a question and answer affair, you will probably want to use some kind of standard questionnaire. The most common type of marketing research is done in such a manner, with the goal of making some kind of sales forecast in specific areas—geographical, sociological, or economic.

The Three Approaches to Research

You have three ways of going about this:

❑ You can use the mail.

❑ You can use the telephone.

❑ You can interview one on one.

These three approaches are strictly up-front research, called "primary" research. There are innumerable offshoots of background research available, called "secondary" research.

For background, you can use government publications of all kinds, or data available from libraries or advertising media in the form of magazines, journals, and trade publications. You can use books of all kinds, too, but don't forget that books tend to be dated.

For sample testing, you can use cities or neighborhoods where people of average income live, especially if they are the typical customer you want to interest in your product or service.

You can also use sales reports of all kinds, and news of sales activity gleaned from publications and newsletters involved in dispensing such information.

To put it succinctly, primary information is hands-on, up-front information that you got yourself. Secondary information is just background information gotten from somewhere else. Both are needed in order to create a clear picture of any marketing scene.

(3) GATHERING THE INFORMATION

The actual gathering of the information is simple enough, once the plan has been set. Let's break up the gathering of informational data into two segments:

❑ secondary information

❑ primary information

We'll take up these two separately.

Gathering Secondary Data

It is usually best to approach the collection of information first from the long-range aspect of secondary data and then from the short-range aspect of primary data.

Secondary data usually exists in printed form of some kind. Good places to locate secondary data include the following:

❑ census tables and reports

❑ trade journals

❑ directories

❑ newsletters

❑ government publications

❑ trade association information

❑ internal company sales reports

❏ newspapers

❏ general circulation magazines

To look at these sources from a slightly different point of view, you should be looking for such information as:

❏ population trends

❏ retail sales activity

❏ industry inventory levels

❏ state of the economy

❏ industry sales figures

❏ disposable personal income

❏ legal developments

❏ IRS changes

There are also a number of studies published by commercial marketing research firms that contain good marketing information on a wide variety of products and services. You can make use of these findings—usually gathered by professional researchers—at a minimal cost for the service.

NOTE: Background data will hardly ever solve any of your important informational needs, but you do want a good "big picture" of the marketing situation as a whole to use as a starting point. Most printed material is, sadly, pretty much out of date. Market changes from day to day are so volatile that the shifts can be stunning even to the experienced merchandiser. On the other hand, the market situation may remain remarkably stable for months. The message is: keep up with the market conditions at all times to make sure you always know exactly what is happening.

The most important thing to remember about secondary data is that it may give you inspirational leads on how to obtain primary data.

That's what we'll take up now.

Gathering Primary Data

Depending on the type of business you are in, you may not need primary data at all. Many business activities can survive on secondary data alone. If you do need primary data, you'll need some kind of program planning, you'll need to study complicated methods of gathering information, and you'll need to know how to get and comprehend in-depth analyses.

A good example of a typical primary study would be a customer survey in which you set out to gather information about consumer desires and expectations first-hand—asking questions formulated to build up a good marketing picture.

There are several easy ways to handle this type of study:

❏ You may simply make a telephone call to a customer and ask the customer whatever questions you want to.

❏ You may send a postcard or letter with two or three basic questions. (To do this, you need only use a regular mailing list.)

You may need more information about consumer attitudes, habits, and preferences. If this is the case, you should make use of some kind of market research firm or consultant. This will cost money, depending on the size and complexity of the survey and on the size and reputation of the market researchers.

Something to keep in mind is that good information is not necessarily the result of expensive research. You can always reduce costs by utilizing some of the more inexpensive market research organizations.

Where to Gather Market Data

There are a number of places you can look to for data that can be gathered inexpensively.

Advertising Agency Research

Large advertising agencies have research departments that handle market surveys. To develop successful and effective advertising campaigns, they have to know all about what consumers are thinking and how the markets for their clients are functioning.

If you have an advertising agency working for your company, put it to work for you, and let its market research unit handle all your problems.

Consultant Help

If you do not have a working relationship with an advertising agency that has a market research department, you can always hire a consultant.

First of all, you must draw up a work plan in order to define the research objective you want to reach. These particulars include a questionnaire to elicit information you want, a general overall plan for taking samplings, and the methodology—by mail, by interview, by observation, by telephone.

Once you have drawn up a plan, hire an independent consultant to review it. There are lists of consultants in professional directories, such as the *American Marketing Association Membership Roster*. You can also get lists from advertising agencies, local universities, or business associates.

If you aren't sure about your plan, you can always check it out with a marketing professor at a local university. Through him or her you may be able to find a consultant you can depend on.

University Programs

Many colleges will help you with consulting and managerial help if you seek it out. Over 500 universities have small-business institutes that serve businesses all through the year.

This is a part of the Small Business Administration. Students, under the supervision of faculty members, work on particular business problems free of charge. In some cases there may be a small fee, but it is usually quite reasonable.

Multi-Client Surveys

You can hire commercial research firms to make major marketing studies for you in conjunction with other work they might be doing. Usually these studies are paid for jointly by the companies using them.

Focus Group Interviews

A new type of tool for the market research specialist is the so-called focus group interview. A focus group is a small number of customers for a particular product or service. This group of people then meets together to discuss a certain product, service, advertising campaign, marketing program, or other subject of interest.

The typical focus group is composed of eight to ten members. It is important that the group be in the hands of a good moderator. Otherwise, it will be a waste of time.

Don't forget that this type of group-think is to be used only for exploratory, brain-storming purposes, and that the information obtained from these interviews cannot be used as conclusive findings. What a focus group decides cannot be extrapolated to the population at large, since the individuals of the group have not been selected with an eye to a balanced educational, social, or economic grouping.

129

(4) TESTING THE MARKET

Before you go ahead and release a questionnaire to a firm doing research for you, be sure to give the questionnaire a rigorous pretesting beforehand. There may be flaws in the wording of a certain question. You may find you are getting information you don't really need, and not getting the information that you do need.

The point of pretesting is to see how the questions work. Are they confusing? Are they ambiguous? Are any too complicated for the respondents?

Use a small pilot study and look carefully at the information you get from your respondents. This is a chance to find out if your questionnaire will actually get the proper information you want, or if you are going to have to figure out a better way to elicit it.

Consolidating the Study

There is a tendency on the part of the entrepreneur making a market study to ask too much, rather than to concentrate on the questions that *really* need to be answered. If you find that your questions wander all over the place, the chances are that you're asking too much. The idea is to keep the questionnaire simple.

Ask only what you want to learn. Work on only one problem at a time in the most clearcut and direct way possible. Keep your questions short and right to the point. Don't ask a lot of extra questions. People get tired of answering questions. The fewer, the better.

(5) FOLLOWING UP THE RESEARCH

No market research study should be a one-time thing. After you have finished making one study, you have achieved temporarily what you set out to do. Nevertheless, the study is not complete. No survey of the market situation is *ever* complete. It goes on from day to day as the market goes on—ever-changing.

As soon as you find the answers to the question you want to ask, you should then begin to draw up a new list of questions, largely inspired by the first series of questions you have asked and had answered.

If you have no new questions to ask, repeat the same ones you asked before. You'll be surprised at how much these answers have changed in that brief interim.

A few questions asked at different points in time can prove more valuable than a lot of questions asked only once and never asked again. Asking questions again and again is the only way you can obtain any kind of picture that shows trends beginning to develop and changes showing a swift market revolution.

Pitfalls in Obtaining Reliable Market Data

Successful market research is a complicated procedure, and it is not surprising that there are a number of major pitfalls you can encounter in trying to accomplish a satisfactory search for pertinent information.

Four major pitfalls:

❏ lack of specific objectives

❏ misapplication of principles and methods

❏ inability to extract pertinent data

❏ absence of reassessments

Lack of Specific Objectives

One of the most serious errors you can commit in attempting to mount a successful market research study is the improper statement and resolution of your specific objectives. You must know ahead of time exactly what you want the study to concentrate on, and you must determine exactly how to expect to accomplish your objective or objectives before you start.

By a careful determination of the exact objectives you have in mind, you build up a good modus operandi for the search itself and in turn establish a starting point of all the following steps.

With those objectives clearly in mind, you can then clarify whatever decisions you are going to come to after the research has been collected. You can also establish the kinds of answers you want in whatever marketing unknowns you are searching for. And you can line up whatever results are to be expected and determine how they are to be used in selling your product or service.

If you do not have a well-defined statement of all your research objectives, you will never be able to get the information you want any more than you will be able to assess that information once you get it.

Misapplication of Principles and Methods

Market research is a complex and confusing operation at best. Even the questionnaire you draw up may be made in such a way that the study shows not what you want it to show, but something else entirely. It is always important to remember that in many cases the way you phrase a question tends to determine the answer you will get.

Because of this problem, you have to repeatedly go over your questionnaire to make sure that each question is clear and that the answer to the question will not be

132

influenced by the wording of the question or the way it is posed.

You should also make sure not only that the questions are all asked properly, but that they are asked in the correct sequence.

There are any number of different research techniques possible in developing a good questionnaire. Each is usually effective in a specific marketing situation. It is up to you to determine what type of method to use for your own situation.

For most small businesses, the mail questionnaire is probably the most satisfactory, because it can be done for less cost than any other type of data collection. Yet in some instances—where, for example, instructions and subtle questions are asked—a mail survey may not be the right one to use at all.

Another problem with a mail survey is its usually low response rate, which can make the entire process of market research ineffective.

Inability to Extract Pertinent Data

Once the questionnaires are answered, it is necessary to study the answers to make sure they are reasonably correct. Usually there is some error involved in any type of measurement. A person who answers a questionnaire may not understand the question correctly; thus there is a chance of error at that point. Even if the question is properly understood, the recipient may not know the actual answer, and may then put down an answer that is not quite true or relevant.

You have to minimize these possibilities by carefully and meticulously studying the results and comparing each questionnaire with the others. Even so, the margin for error can be extremely high in the final result.

Absence of Reassessments

The marketplace is a dynamic environment. Economic conditions are in a state of constant flux. Hidden variables can affect the situation on a day-to-day basis. Competition can surge or vanish. Government regulations can alter conditions drastically in twenty-four hours.

Yet market research is a one-time thing only, much like a photograph. A still picture never really shows the movement and action of a person or thing; it takes a motion picture to show that. Marketing is movement and action. One study does not tell nearly enough about what is going on; it merely measures what was going on at a particular moment in history.

Market research must be an ongoing procedure, with constant reassessments necessary. Never forget that even the most effective and best-intentioned survey can be outdated due to any number of variables that can throw off the results by light-years.

In no way does the fact that you may stumble in your market research mean that you should not try to make such a study—even if you are far from an experienced and seasoned professional. Nevertheless, you should know what kind of problems you may encounter that could make you stumble in your work.

Most of the problems mentioned can be in a large part dodged by careful planning and careful assessment of data that comes in through all the research activities initiated in a study.

The answer is not to spend a great deal of money with a time-tested and crack team of research experts, for it does not necessarily follow that spending a great deal of money will improve or even guarantee perfect results.

You get the best market research from carefully planning the study from the beginning. You get the best results by identifying your goals in advance, and you must make sure that the research methods you use or that you instruct someone else to use are tailored to your own needs for specific information so that you will get valid and reliable results that will help you in marketing *your* product or service.

You have to weigh potential benefits of the information you collect against the cost of obtaining it. That is true no matter how much you spend. It is best to begin by using the easiest and least expensive means of getting that information.

If you are in need of a more complex survey, it will usually pay off to bring in professional help from the outside.

In the long run, each case is an individual one. You must find out what your own needs are in regards to your own particular marketing problems.

9

Promoting a Business

This segment could be called "A Tale of Two Cities." What particular cities they are shouldn't matter at first. It's what the cities did to counteract economic difficulties deemed insurmountable at the time that is important.

Both cities are located in the United States on opposite sides of the continent. And both cities are no longer ghost towns, which they could easily have become if they had not found the magic key to turn adversity into prosperity.

How did they do it?

By intelligence, ingenuity, and a lot of good luck.

But—most especially—by using the proper type of *basic promotion.*

THE TALE OF THE FIRST CITY

It was the turn of the century and America was prospering. At least, certain parts were making out sensationally well. Other parts were drying up and vanishing overnight —like the buffalo. Although the westward expansion had more or less run its course, there were communities hanging in out there in the West. And just barely hanging in.

Ghost towns were springing up throughout that region. Many of these towns originally had been created to support working mines of gold, silver, and copper, but had died as the mineral veins petered out.

There were communities established along the coast, but there was little trade there. Most of the western country was given over to agriculture, but the vast distance between the West and the East—where most of the consumers lived—prevented any important increase in marketing possibilities.

Produce Galore but No Consumers

In short, the area was languishing. Marketing was presented with a classic impasse:

❑ There was potential for a huge increase in the production of agricultural products.

❑ The lack of customers within reaching distance precluded any development or expansion.

In short, what the coastal communities needed more than anything else was a lot more transplants from the East. Most people were happy to live on the civilized eastern seaboard, where there were good jobs available, and where the living was already made easier by fully developed towns and cities.

Even those lured to the coast by free train rides (which took days) were less than impressed when they got there. To them the whole area, excluding San Francisco, looked like a wasteland. There were no big trees, no rolling landscapes lush with foliage, no lakes and beautiful fertile plains.

The Image of a Vast Desert

Something had to be done to change the image of the place. If the image was that of a burning, sandy desert, an extended Death Valley all the way from the middle of the state down to the Mexican border, then the developers of Southern California would have to change that image.

How to do it?

Obviously, the entrepreneurs in the area reasoned, by making the image one of fertility, of green, of shade, of coolness, and of luxurious peace. The idea was to make the place look like the Garden of Eden. Of course, if Eden couldn't be managed, at least the place should look like some kind of garden.

It was difficult to make flowers grow with the current shortage of water, but with the proper irrigation of the area through reservoirs of water miles from the area, it could be done. And once the desert areas were provided with water, they did begin to turn into gardens. Everything soon was coming up roses.

Promises of That Rose Garden

The state fairs held in the region showed huge examples of excellent produce—proving that the area could be turned into a garden—but only local people visited the fair grounds. Something had to be initiated to attract people from outside, people who would see the place and decide to pull up roots in the East and stay in the West.

A World's Fair?

Too costly.

How about a parade? A parade of flowers?

Why not?

138

But who would come to see the parade? A parade was a secondary thing, subservient to the celebration of the Fourth of July, or Labor Day, or—something. If the parade could be managed, there had to be something for the parade to commemorate.

A game?

A contest?

A race?

Baseball was all the rage at the turn of the century, but the big teams were all well entrenched east of the Mississippi, and traveling was difficult even from New York to Chicago. No team could be enticed into journeying all the way out to the West Coast.

There was always football, but that was an elitist sport, played only in the Ivy League colleges and a few of the big land-grant colleges in the Midwest. And yet . . .

Competition Between Regions

If the local colleges on the West Coast could be persuaded to send a contender, and if the Midwest colleges, which were near enough to make the trip without excessive discomfort, were willing, why not a contest between the best of the West Coast colleges and the best of—say— the midwestern land-grant colleges?

The obvious time for such a competition would be at the end of the year after the regular season was finished and the winners of the specific areas decided. Christmas? New Year's? Why not New Year's? And, given the contest, the parade would celebrate the big game between East (really Midwest) and West.

Because of the year-round quality of the weather in California, the parade would be able to feature the flowers of the area, showing what kind of a marvelous garden the countryside was—even in the dead of winter. A parade of flowers?

No.

A parade of roses.

139

And, of course, the after-season football game would take its name from the flowers on display. The Flower Game? The Rose Game? No. Flower Game didn't sound right. Neither did Rose Game.

The game would be played in a nearby stadium built for the event. But even Flower Stadium didn't sound right. Well how about calling the stadium a "bowl" from its shape—to hold not only the players and the customers, but the flowers as well?

The Flower Bowl. The Rose Bowl.

A play on words.

The First of the Bowl Games

In 1902 the first game was played in Pasadena—and, as they say, the rest is history. The point of the story is not that football history was made, but that promotion history was made.

The real purpose of the project was to change the image of Southern California as an endless desert to that of an endless garden. The football contest was simply a part of the scheme to show off Southern California as an eternal garden of roses.

The floats of flowers were important, but only important as a device to focus interest on the flowers that made them up.

THE TALE OF THE SECOND CITY

The second city had virtually the same problem as the first city. It too was languishing economically. It too needed a shot in the arm. It too needed visitors to spend money and settle down there.

The second city was on the East Coast, where there were plenty of people already. Although a beach community, this city could not attract enough crowds to fill the beaches and fill the coffers of the tourist-oriented businesses.

Swimming was popular, but not popular enough to entice people of all ages. The boardwalk was popular, but not popular enough. Business was declining rather than rising. People were spending their vacations in the mountains and at nearby lakes rather than on the seashore.

How to change the public image of the boardwalk?

Beauties in Bathing Suits

It was no secret that bathing at the beaches was popular among the young men because of the young women in bathing suits. In the early 1920s the bathing suits were getting smaller and smaller and the women were showing more and more of their arms and legs and shoulders and whatever.

Not all women were beauties, but who cared? Many of them were.

And so, thought one entrepreneur, why not assemble all the beauties in bathing suits to see who was the *most* beautiful? In fact, by assembling them at Atlantic City, perhaps that would attract other bathers and even tourists to the area to watch the bathing beauties as they paraded about to be judged by connoisseurs of the female form.

The Cult of the Body Beautiful

The first Miss America Contest was held in 1921, and from that time on, the cult of the female form in the bathing suit has become part of the American scene. The contest was successful from the first and soon thereafter other contests were established at almost every beach in the country, with the rules pretty much the same. Al-

141

though the predominant idea of the contest was to select the most beautiful woman in a bathing suit, it was the long parade of women in those suits that drew the crowds.

It also precipitated imitations by young women who were not in the contests. They too began to wear skimpier and skimpier suits in order to expose their figures— which of course was not in any way distasteful to the men on the beaches. Many men flocked to the beaches just to watch the women. Swimming became an accepted fad. Sun-tanning became another accepted fad—and the beaches began to prosper once more.

So did the boardwalk and the businesses and workers around the boardwalk.

The Way to Get Press Coverage

Promotion, any way you look at it. The effort was to bring more people to the beaches, which on their own were unable to generate enthusiasm or induce people to spend much money. The beauty contest was simply a ploy to attract the press.

Once the press had the pictures, then the people saw the pictures, recognized the attraction of bathing beauties, and came to the beaches to watch and to swim—and to spend more.

The bathing beauty contests at Atlantic City succeeded as well as the Rose Parade and the Rose Bowl. Both plans aroused interest in areas that seemed to be dying on the vine. Both plans succeeded in bringing people to specific places that were not too popular.

The important thing to note is that in each case the promotional ploy initiated to bring people in was a diversion from the actual target. In Pasadena, the target was to change the image of the area. In Atlantic City, the target was to attract crowds to the boardwalk. Both targets of course involved the eventual making of money from those who were attracted there.

142

Nevertheless, the actual promotional gimmick was decidedly subservient to the actual *purpose*.

The Two Prongs of Publicity

Promotion is usually a two-pronged tool. To promote an enterprise of any kind, you should use both prongs. They are:

❑ advertising

❑ publicity

Although you might think advertising and publicity are pretty much the same thing, this is not true at all. There are many differences, the two most significant are:

❑ advertising is paid for

❑ publicity is free

Advertising can be molded to your own particular needs, and it can be totally controlled because it is that part of promotion that you pay directly for. Publicity—or public relations, as it is called in more stately and grandiose terms—is more subtle and complex and can be confusing at times. Let's take up advertising first.

A Look at General Advertising

There are many different ways to advertise a product, a service, or a store or shop. You can plan a campaign for millions of dollars to include television advertising, national magazine advertising, newspaper advertising, and throwaway leaflets of all kinds. You can also establish a direct-mail campaign to sell something.

For the average entrepreneur just starting out, however, the picture is slightly different. Advertising simply

143

means getting the word out to other people that you have a product or a service or a store that everyone should know about.

There are seven steps in getting out an advertising message about a product or a service. They are:

(1) Word of mouth.

(2) Letters or fliers.

(3) Bulletin boards.

(4) Telephone messages.

(5) Direct mail.

(6) Classified ads.

(7) Display ads.

(8) Electronic media.

(1) Word of Mouth

The first step is to get the word out about yourself and your product or service among your closest neighbors. You can do this in the simplest fashion possible: just go to your neighbors and tell them what you are doing. If you can interest someone close by you in your product or service, you then become known for that product or service, and others learn about it.

(2) Letters or Fliers

The second step is to back up the word of mouth about you—and your own personal campaign to introduce yourself to potential customers—with a letter or flier of some kind telling about your product or service in specific terms, including, among others, your address, kind of work, and price range.

This type of solicitation is a little like direct-mail promotion. Your letter or flier is an indirect advertising pitch, telling what you are up to.

(3) Bulletin Boards

The third step is to go out a little further and make your pitch on the bulletin boards in adjoining areas. You know where most of the community bulletin boards are located. In addition to mailing your letters and handing them out, pin them up in any public place you can find. Super-markets and churches usually have community bulletin boards; use them.

(4) Telephone Messages

The fourth step is to resort to the telephone. The tele-phone is not a primary method of advertising, but is usually used as a follow-up, or back-up, to other methods. Use it as a corollary to a mailed or distributed leaflet.

Be advised, however, that telephone solicitation is a big bore to most people. Don't be surprised if many people hang up on you in mid-sentence. You have to have an ingratiating manner—and luck as well—to make a sale or pitch by phone.

(5) Direct Mail

The fifth step is to try direct-mail solicitation. If you've already used the mails for step two, simply vary your pitch a little, and spread it out geographically. Your first mailings were close to you; a direct-mail solicitation should spread the word in a widening circle from your neighborhood.

Your product or service may also lend itself to solicita-tion by direct mail; that is, you may want to sell your product or service at a distance. In direct mail you can control your expenses, you can control your targets, and you get immediate contact and an answer to your pitch. Nevertheless, you have to remember that direct mail is to most people "junk mail" and has a bad image. Also, be sure you use up-to-date lists to get the best results.

(6) Classified Ads

The sixth step is to try the classified ads in your local publications; they are usually fairly inexpensive. A classified ad is not a surefire seller, however. Many people never look at the classified sections, but it is a good window for the advertising approach.

(7) Display Ads

The seventh step is to try a small ad in a local newspaper. It all depends on what kind of product or service you are selling. You may find that your best results come from a small newspaper ad. On the other hand, you may find advertising in this fashion is a waste of time and money. You'll never know unless you try.

(8) Electronic Media

For the beginning entrepreneur, the eighth step will probably be sometime in the future. That move is to try out electronic advertising, which because of its cost is generally considered "big time." Although a small business may use local radio advertising to good effect, even that tends to be costly for the newly established enterprise. In spite of the "big-time" aspect of electronic advertising, it should be considered an important step when an entrepreneur decides he or she is doing well, but could do better on a wider scale.

Now let's take a few examples of different types of advertising and examine how they work.

The Small-Space Advertising Ploy

With the recent rise in the numbers of individual entrepreneurs, there has been an increasing interest in what has come to be called "small-space advertising." This refers to certain specific types of inexpensive advertising, whose cost can be controlled easily. There are a couple of good reasons why small-space advertising has grown so rapidly in the past few years.

Most of the trouble in advertising has been caused by the astronomical costs of television exposure. Only huge companies with enormous advertising budgets can afford television ads—even local ones.

The rise of television advertising caused a decrease in magazine advertising, which had been the most costly type of national advertising. This decrease resulted in the demise of a number of general circulation magazines— big circulators like *Life, Look, Saturday Evening Post,* and *Colliers* (although *Life* and the *Saturday Evening Post* still appear in reincarnated but truncated form).

When the mass magazine died, a new phenomenon developed: the weekly tabloids circulated in supermarkets on a nationwide basis. These tabloids couldn't attract big national advertisers, and so they opened their columns to classified ads, to small-space display ads, and to mail-order ads.

There are a number of important outlets for small-space advertising. They occur in newspapers, in magazines, and in the yellow pages of the telephone book. Let's take up these three media independently, starting with newspapers.

NEWSPAPER ADVERTISING

To begin with, there are a number of different types of newspapers, including national newspapers, regional newspapers, local newspapers, and shoppers (also called throwaways).

A national newspaper like the *Wall Street Journal, USA Today,* or the *Christian Science Monitor* can reach people in all parts of the country, unlike the *Miami Herald,* which tends to be sold only in the Miami area of Florida.

Newspapers can also be categorized according to their frequency of publication. The genuine "daily"—like the

New York Times—appears every day of the week, holiday or not. The *Sunday New York Times* is a slightly different proposition, since it includes supplements and fillers that are not offered during weekdays.

Other newspapers, like the national tabloids, are published only once every week. The same is true of regional newspapers of one kind or another, and many small, very local regional newspapers serving thinly populated areas of the country.

As an advertiser, you can opt for any one of these types of newspaper to circulate your message throughout any given area.

Six Kinds of Ads

Generally speaking, there are five different kinds of advertising you can use in a typical newspaper if you are an individual proprietor and not interested in full-page display advertising. Here are the various categories of small-space advertising:

❏ display advertising

❏ classified advertising

❏ classified-display combination advertising

❏ contingency advertising

❏ per-inquiry advertising

❏ mail-order advertising

(1) Display Advertising

As the individual proprietor of a shop or a business, you may find a small display-type advertisement exactly what you need to make people aware of your product or service. (If your shop grows and becomes a department store, you can of course avail yourself of a full-page advertisement in order to feature all the bargains or lines you are carrying in your store.)

If you are advertising a one-person service, you can pick as small an ad as you wish. The newspaper may even help you write the ad if you are unfamiliar with the way it is done. The bigger you are, of course, the more important your ad pitch is. You may even choose to hire an advertising agency to handle all the nitty-gritty. Then all you have to do is supervise the writing and production of the ad.

Display advertising can run in size all the way from a full page down to an advertisement one column in width by one inch in height. You can find out what is available by talking to the advertising manager of the newspaper.

Don't forget the national tabloids or national newspapers when you are thinking of advertising. The situation is exactly the same. Most will sell small display ad spaces to you.

(2) Classified Advertising

For the very small individual proprietor, you can always use the classified advertising columns. Some classified columns allow you to buy an inch of space, or even more. In this way your ad will stand out from all the rest.

Classified advertising is ideally suited to the very small entrepreneur who has a product or service and wants to let it be known to the public. Of course, no classified ad is as prominent or gets as much attention as a regular display ad, no matter what its size.

(3) Classified-Display Combination

You can always avail yourself of a kind of expanded classified ad that resembles a very small display advertisement, but is located in the classified columns. This is technically a combination of classified and display advertising. Its advantage is that it shows up remarkably well in the middle of eye-deadening columns of classified ads.

The price is a little higher than a regular classified ad, but it is worth it to have the attractive larger letters and more white space.

(4) Contingency Advertising

Many shoppers have classified columns of items for sale in which you do not pay anything for the insertion of an advertisement, but do pay a percentage of the amount of the item you sell. For the average entrepreneur in business on a day-to-day basis, the one-shot contingency ad is not particularly effective or even apropos.

(5) Per-Inquiry Advertising

For the entrepreneur trying to market a new product or service, the PI—or "per inquiry"—ad may be the answer. You can draw up and publish an advertisement under this arrangement at no significant cost, although there may be a small service charge.

You will be billed for the number of inquiries that your advertisement draws. For that reason, most PI ads contain write-in coupons or some inducement to write in for a free catalogue or brochure.

The newspaper tabulates the number of inquiries that come in, and then bills you for the number it receives. You are then given the inquiries to respond to or fulfill. If the advertisement is a big success, you will pay more than if it is a failure. If no inquiries at all come in, you probably will not be charged except for the base fee if there is one.

(6) Mail-Order Advertising

One of the most effective and successful of all newspaper advertisements used by entrepreneurs trying to get a business of some kind going is the mail-order ad. There are several instant advantages a mail-order ad has over any other kind. In fact, it is one of the oldest forms of advertising going.

What makes a mail-order ad stand out immediately is either an obvious clip-out coupon in the lower right-hand corner, or the familiar words:

Send For Our Free Booklet!

The response to a mail-order ad is immediate. As soon as the newspaper hits the streets, you get response or you get no response. This is particularly effective for an entrepreneur who is starting out and wants to sell by mail. You get an inquiry, you get the money, and you send your product to the buyer.

Main Elements of Mail-Order Advertising

The typical mail-order ad is concerned with five elements:

❑ It features a product.

❑ It describes the product.

❑ It may picture the product.

❑ It exhorts the reader to sign the coupon and clip it out to send in.

❑ It may ask for money.

You can use a mail-order ad to sell a product or service, to tease the reader into sending for a booklet for information about you or your product or service (which secures names and addresses for direct-mail lists), or to urge the reader to send in for a catalogue or sales listing.

Development of Print Media Strategy

Repetition is the key to successful advertising. The first time you heard the phrase "Where's the beef?" you didn't rush out of the house to buy a hamburger at the nearest Wendy's. However, by the tenth time you heard it, or by the hundredth, you may well have had the urge to go out and get a hamburger. It is the repetition of the phrase that begins to make you salivate.

"How do you spell relief?" When you heard it the first

time, it was a simple question. By the hundredth time you heard it, your stomach was churning.

Because repetition—not size—is really the crux of advertising success, you should try to find out the maximum efficacy of repetition, that is, how often you should repeat your message in a specific period of time.

The Three Approaches to Ad Campaigns

In fact, there are three basic approaches to setting up an advertising campaign of any kind. These approaches have to do with the pattern of repetition, rather than simply with the frequency of repetition.

These are the three:

❏ the continuous campaign

❏ the seasonal campaign

❏ the flighting campaign

The Continuous Campaign

If your business continues throughout the year on a regular basis, you should be satisfied with a schedule of advertising that includes a routine and steady pattern of ad insertions. You may have two in June, two in July, and so on all through the year. This will afford you a continuous campaign of image-making in the public eye.

The Seasonal Campaign

If your business does not run on a regular basis, but tends to have certain regular seasons—the holidays, for example, or certain climatic periods—then you should use the seasonal approach. Your ads will then appear during the pre-Christmas season, perhaps, and through the pre-Easter season, and so on. You schedule your ads for these periods, and ignore the in-between months.

The Flighting Campaign

If your business is especially flighty—that is, only has one or two *big* seasons during the year (an income tax accountant, for example)—then you use what is called a "flighting" approach to the ad campaign. You insert all your ads one after the other in rapid-fire machine-gun order just before and during your big season.

In addition to frequency of timing, you can also scale down certain insertions and scale up others, perhaps building in size for five days before your big season, or whatever. This all depends on what your business is, and how you want to approach advertising it.

MAGAZINE ADVERTISING

Magazine advertising tends to be a great deal more expensive than newspaper advertising, especially advertising in a national glossy-paper magazine that is consumer-oriented with a circulation in the millions.

Nevertheless, you may find affordable room in magazines for some mail-order advertising or small display advertising, particularly in the back of consumer magazines.

They Stay Alive Longer

Remember that each issue of a magazine is longer-lived than a newspaper issue, so consequently a mail-order ad in a magazine has a much longer life than one in a newspaper. For that reason, the extra money you put into a mail-order magazine ad may be well spent. Someone may pick up the magazine many weeks from the cover date, see your ad, and buy something from you.

153

Another factor to keep in mind is circulation. If your own local newspaper has a circulation of 50,000, and is a daily paper, you can see that by putting the same ad in a magazine with a circulation of 6,000,000 that you'll be getting about 120 times the coverage! If it only costs 100 times as much, you're going to get more of the bang for the buck.

Magazine advertising can be a tricky business. Ads must be prepared months ahead of time. Sales dates usually precede the month of the issue sometimes by two months.

THE YELLOW PAGES

Many would-be advertisers tend to make a major mistake in developing an advertising campaign: they forget about the yellow pages in the telephone book. If you are an entrepreneur who is trying to get your name in front of the public, never sell the yellow pages short. Although no one will see your ad in the book simply by thumbing through the directory, if someone wants your particular product or service, he or she will find you there.

If newspapers are quick, and magazines are slow in response time—then the yellow pages are total slow motion. But the potential for year-round business exists, and for future years as well if you take out an ad in each year's yellow pages.

You can get one-line entries, or display advertisements as large as you want. The only catch is that the ad must appear in its proper niche in the yellow-page alphabetical breakdown of subjects.

—And Then There's Publicity

The second prong of the two-pronged tool of promotion is publicity. Advertising is a fairly cut-and-dried affair, with advertising campaigns and schedules assuming major import, and total control in the hands of the advertiser.

Publicity is in no way cut and dried. In many cases it is almost as subtle as an undercover operation. As you can see by examining the invention of the Rose Bowl at Pasadena and the invention of the bathing beauty contest at Atlantic City, publicity is not as obvious or aboveboard as advertising. A pitchman may be working both prongs of the promotion tool—advertising and publicity—but the game played in publicity is more complicated and arcane than that played in advertising.

Publicity is defined as news or information about a product, service, or idea that is published in some form on behalf of a company or sponsor but is not paid for by the person sponsoring it. Publicity goes hand-in-glove with advertising to help achieve what are called the "public relations" aims of a company or proprietor. You must utilize both to make promotion effective.

The Difference Is Story Value

There is one key difference between an advertising story and a publicity story. The advertising story can be a simple explication of a product, a service, or a basic idea. The publicity story must have a news or information value before an editor or program director will let it appear in print or on the air.

And that key difference spells out one of the main problems of getting publicity. You can see immediately that since publicity must have news value its appearance is completely at the discretion of an editor or program director. In other words, the space or time is not for sale the way advertising space or time is. Publicity space or time is free to the proprietor or sponsor, but the sponsor bears the cost and effort of making up the story that becomes the publicity in the first place. As in the Pasadena and Atlantic City stories, the sponsor may not be readily apparent to reader, viewer, or listener—only the sponsor's subliminal message.

If advertising can be readily purchased, why should you bother to use publicity to back up a strong advertising campaign?

It's a simple one-word answer.

CREDIBILITY

Write that on a three-by-five card and put it in your bathroom mirror to look at every day. No promotion succeeds if it lacks an inner core of credibility.

The Built-In Suspicion of Advertising

Because America has had a history of snake-oil salesmen, pitchmen, and con artists of all kinds, most people are automatically suspicious of any kind of advertising. As an average consumer of print or broadcast media, you automatically *think* pitch when an advertisement or commercial appears. Test yourself sometime if you don't believe that.

When you think *pitch*, you immediately put up sales resistance. Your hackles rise, as the saying goes. You begin to try to pick holes in the argument of the pitch-person. And you usually succeed. That is the reason many ads nowadays are couched in humor. Humor is an offbeat approach and is able to worm its way into your consciousness in a sympathetic way without arousing antagonism; it tempts you to let down the barriers of resistance. If you are wooed and if you laugh, the pitch-person has the game half won.

The Integrity of Spokespeople

Enough of that. Indeed advertising, while it is necessary and while it can be controlled, and while it can sell millions of dollars worth of products and services, simply does not arouse a person's interest or instantly stimulate credibility in a product or service.

However, if a new product or a new service receives attention from a reporter or columnist writing material in a newspaper or magazine that is not in any way related to the advertising columns, then you almost automatically tend to *believe* what you are reading. The reason you read a columnist or pundit in the first place is to receive unbiased information—or at least information that has been filtered through the critical faculties of a sympathetic person who is not a part of the team pitching the information.

This objective person is a spokesperson chosen by you as a reader to render decisions on upcoming products or services, more or less giving you the benefit of unprejudiced advice.

Thus the integrity of the spokesperson—who is not paid by an advertising agency or company to push a product—tends to convince you more readily than the words in a paid-for advertisement.

The Myth of Unbiased Objectivity

Even though columnists and editorial writers are as skewed as anyone else, the public's perception is that the written columns in a newspaper or magazine (the "news" columns in newspaper parlance) are objective and unbiased. That lends the material that appears there instant credibility—as positive recognition value.

For this reason alone, it is true that one inch of publicity is worth a hundred inches of advertising, at least from a standpoint of credibility, believability, and recognition value.

NOTE: That does *not* mean that advertising has no place in the media. It *does* have its purpose for the value of its repetition, if nothing else. It also helps build up a total recognition value, over and above that afforded by a publicity drop.

The Basic Types of Publicity

Publicity can take on many different forms, and can appear in all the media—as print in newspapers, journals, magazines, periodicals, newsletters, direct-mail pitches; as visuals in television; and as sound on radio.

Here are the main types of publicity stories:

❏ news release

❏ feature article

❏ press conference

❏ film

❏ video tape

❏ editorial

❏ column material

Let's take them up one by one.

News Release

The news release is the most commonly featured type of straight publicity. Also called the press release, this type of story is widely used in print journalism, in newspapers and in magazines. A typical publicity release usually consists of no more than 300 words of typed copy, perhaps a photograph or line drawing, a fact sheet on the product or service, and the name, address, and phone number of the person to call for further information.

A news release must be of enough story value or in some way helpful to the publication's reader in order to be considered for use.

Feature Article

The feature article is simply a more extended and detailed story about a company, about someone in a company, about the company's processes, or about its overall personnel. Unlike a news release, the article runs from 500 to 3,000 words in length, and contains a great deal more factual material.

The feature article must be written in a manner that makes it readable and pertinent to the publication's readership. For example, a story about marketing a product in some special way might be written for an advertising or marketing magazine, not for a general circulation magazine.

Press Conference

A press conference differs from a news release or a feature article in that the story itself is not written by the company or by someone working for the company being publicized. The actual story will be written by a reporter of the newspaper or magazine attending the press conference.

The conference itself is an assemblage of editors, writers, and program directors invited to hear a major announcement or the release of a special news story that the company has to communicate. Representatives of management are present to make the announcement and to answer reporters' questions. A press kit is usually distributed to the reporters and program directors. The press kit is a "package" of information about the company and the product that can be referred to when the reporter is back at the office preparing the story.

Film

A large company often prepares a visual history of the firm for background information to newcomers, to potential clients, and to anyone else who might want information about it. A film of this sort may be of any length, from five minutes to sixty minutes. For purposes of television use, such a film should be only a five-minute clip or less. Many media specialists feel your clip should run exactly thirty seconds or a minute. However, a program director may remove a section of a larger film for inclusion with whatever news event has been staged.

Video Tape

Information about a company may also be prepared on video tape for showing on the air. The rules for video tapes are exactly the same as the rules for making background films.

Editorial

An editorial is a story written by someone in a company to state a particular position or to refute an opposite position. Currently, most editorial pages of large newspapers contain "op-ed" pages where opposing editorials appear refuting material in the paper's editorial columns. While the use of an editorial as it is written may be rare, an editorial writer for a publication may ask for background material from the company. Such a "backgrounder" should always be available for immediate submission.

Column Material

Like the op-ed story, publicity may appear as a column rather than as a feature article. The difference is that a column is usually written by a known writer or signed by someone's name—whether real or ghost doesn't matter. When material is submitted to a columnist for possible inclusion, it is simply background stuff, possibly with a news peg or suggested editorial slant. The columnist makes use of whatever material appeals and dumps what does not.

What Makes a Story Newsworthy

There are many kinds of stories. Not all of them constitute *news* stories. A story about a particular service you perform may seem to be exciting stuff to you as an individual, but it may leave an editor or writer stifling a yawn. News is a particularly tricky commodity.

The hardest part of providing publicity is to find a story that has a real news angle to it so that it won't look like the publicity it actually is. Getting the news "peg" (as it is called in editorial circles) to hang the story on is always difficult and sometimes impossible. The news peg is the raison d'être of a story—the active ingredient that makes it live.

What News Is—and Isn't

Don't forget that newspapers, magazines, television, and radio are all in the business of communicating *news* to the public. You must study your newspapers, read your magazines, watch your television stations, and listen to your radio outlets in order to find out what news is—and, just as important, what news isn't. Note that not only the guts of the story, the news peg, but the *way it is written* is important.

For a preliminary exercise, go through your local newspaper and read every single item in it. The main stories are obviously printed due to the importance of the news. It's the smaller stories that you should look at carefully. Detect the particular reason each story has been printed—or at least establish a sensible rationale for each story's having been run.

The Human Interest Factor

This old saw provides a good angle on the essentiality of news:

> If a dog bites a man, that's not news. But if a man bites a dog—that's news!

Nevertheless, it isn't always the outré or the bizarre story that is memorable. It may be something quiet and low-keyed. The story may deal with the touch of human warmth and kindness. In fact, the very best story you can produce—the one that will have the most sympathetic readership and be remembered the longest—is the human interest story.

Of course, every story has some human interest in it, but it is astonishing that many do not deal specifically in human interest. People read non-human-interest stories, but they do not remember them as well as they do human interest stories. Every newspaper editor knows this and uses it as a rule of thumb to guide him or her in judging a story's potential.

It is the emotional appeal in the human interest story that sells it to the reader. If the story warms the cockles of the human heart, it has appeal. If the story makes the reader feel good inside, it has appeal. When a story hits the reader where he or she lives, then it is a successful story.

How to Find Stories with Emotional Appeal

There are a number of common subjects that are usually successful in getting under the reader's skin in the right way. You could almost make up a list of these yourself. The most time-tested and effective of these are:

162

❑ animals doomed to die

❑ old folks struggling against adversity

❑ people who do heroic things

❑ children

❑ losers who have fought their way back

❑ any unselfish deed

❑ babies

❑ weddings

❑ love stories

❑ the ironies of life

The trick is to know how to use these subjects in a story that will be turned toward your own business or company in order to give it a part of the reflected emotional appeal of the story itself. And you must never forget that no matter how good a story is, nobody is going to know anything about it *unless you tell them!*

Business Angles That Can Be Used

You don't have to watch a man biting a dog in order to get a story in the papers. Take a look around you at the company you run or at your own individual proprietorship. Surely there are occurrences and events connected with your business enterprise that are newsworthy items.

For example, there are a lot of ways in which to interest a newspaper in printing a story about any business.

Ground-Breaking Ceremonies

Obviously, the opening of a new store or new company is a story in itself. Even if you're expanding or adding on a new wing, you can always get a story out of it. If you can invite the mayor or other politicians to a ceremony honoring the event, then you have a natural press break.

Appointment of New Personnel

If you hire a new employee, you can always manage to get a story. If you take on a new partner, a new manager, or a new official of any kind, you have a potential personality story that is newsworthy in itself.

Announcement of New Models

If you are bringing out a new model of a product, or a streamlined version of a service, that's a story too. It's the announcement of the newness that is the key to the story. This is a chance for you to provide pictures, too. A story with a picture has a much higher recognition factor than a story without, and has a better chance of being used by an editor.

Contests

A contest is usually a publicity stunt in itself. But a contest always appeals to the public—they want to win! It's a story that has news value. If you have a follow-up contest, you can always reprise the first contest by reminiscing about the winners, and what they did with their winnings.

Gifts to Charities

In a slow season, you can always establish a story by giving a special gift to a worthwhile charity. The charity doesn't have to be tied up with your business in any way. It's the gift itself that makes the news. It's not unlikely that you can get a good heartwarming story out of the services of the charity to get your company a little bit of reflected glory.

Putting the Story Together

There are two basic ways in which you can prepare a story idea for the press—and that includes both print media and broadcast media.

❑ You can write the story in the form of a press release and send it to the newspaper or television station.

❑ You can invite the press to come to your store to cover the story there during a press conference.

When you write the story, it is considered a release. When you invite the press to your place, the invitation is considered a pitch, or tip sheet.

The Press Release: Specifics

Here are some special elements you should pay attention to when you are writing your own press release:

(1) Identify your company, yourself, and your story—in a brief "keynote" of a few sentences, no more—on the first page.

(2) Include a release date on the first page in the upper right hand corner—the day you want the story to run.

(3) Double-space the copy, leaving an inch-and-a-half margin on either side of the page, top and bottom, and don't end a page in the middle of a paragraph.

(4) Use white typewriting paper, 8½ x 11 inches, typing on only one side of each sheet. Give the editor the original or a photocopy, never a carbon.

(5) On succeeding pages use a "slug" line, or short identification phrase, in the top corner. Under that write "add 1," "add 3," and so on.

(6) Put "more" at the bottom of each page until the last one. At the end, put "###."

(7) Begin the story halfway down the first page, and five or six lines down on succeeding pages.

(8) In writing the story be sure to adhere to the old-fashioned newspaper formula of the five "Ws": that it tells who, what, when, where, and why.

(9) Indent all paragraphs five spaces.

(10) Include a key paragraph in the release that conveys the "message" of your company or product—a statement that parallels your standard advertising pitch.

(11) Make sure all photographs submitted are 8 x 10 glossies, cropped exactly as you want them to appear. Submit only high contrast, very clear black-and-white pictures.

(12) Include captions with all photographs. Captions must be attached to photographs, so as not to be lost.

(13) On the news release include the name of a spokesperson who can be contacted to provide further information.

(14) With the news release include a cover letter that introduces your project and cites its significance. Make this a brief pitch letter that will entice the editor to read further.

(15) At the end of the cover letter, offer to schedule interviews if the newspaper editor wants them.

Writing a New-Product Release

For the entrepreneur with a new product for sale there is no more effective way of promoting that product than to use what publications call the new-product columns. In these columns free publicity is always available for a product that is genuinely *new*, interesting, and practicable.

If you decide to prepare a new-product release, you should at first check through all the magazines you want to send your release in order to determine whether they run such columns. At one time all magazines used new-product columns. Now not all do. The best way to find out is to check through the magazines in question at your local library.

In some cases, instructions are given for your benefit. In most magazines, however, there are no instructions.

A new-product release is composed of three parts:

❑ a short news release

❑ a photograph of the product

❑ a caption attached to the photograph

Short News Release

The short news release should give an accurate, detailed description of your product. You should type this release on company letterhead stationery, or type in your name, address, and name of the company on the top of the sheet of paper. The copy should be double-spaced, with a one-inch margin on both sides of the paper.

Write the copy so that the important information comes at the beginning, with the lesser information at the end. The editor may cut off the end for space purposes. At the same time, be sure to use the "who, what, when, where, and why" rule.

NOTE: Don't write this copy like an advertisement. Lay off the hard sell. Play it very cool and objective. The product and the idea of the product should be strong enough to sell itself.

Photograph of the Product

The photograph should be a black and white, high contrast glossy showing the product off in good fashion. The size can be 4 x 5, 5 x 7, or 8 x 10. Be sure a professional photographer takes the picture.

You can put your company name in the photograph, but keep it discreet so it can be taken out if the editor doesn't want it to show. Some magazines have a rule against that kind of plugging.

Caption Attached to the Photograph

In the caption, identify the product with a telling but brief caption. In many cases, the publication may use only the photograph and caption, without using the news release at all. All pertinent information should be condensed in the caption in a punchy fashion.

Start typing the caption halfway down the sheet of paper. Identify your company by name and address. Type the caption immediately below—short and concise.

To get an idea of how such a caption should read, take a look at a typical new-product release in a magazine. The style of writing and the way to make the pitch will become apparent.

When the caption is typed, place it underneath the photograph. Attach the caption sheet to the photograph with Scotch tape, and fold the caption so it covers the lower half of the photograph.

Mailing Out a New-Product Release

Put the release, the photograph, and the caption in a manila envelope with a strong cardboard backing to protect the photo, and mail it to the magazine in care of the New-Products Editor.

You are allowed to send the same packet to any

number of magazines. But make sure that you send out all your releases at the same time. No magazine wants to be late by six months after everybody else has used your product release.

Check List for Writing Publicity Copy

Although you may consider yourself effective in your writing, you may not be able to write truly salesworthy copy. Here are a few questions you should ask yourself after you have completed your publicity story—be it a short release, a feature article, or a longer backgrounder.

❑ Is the copy lively enough? Or does it put the reader to sleep?

❑ Does the copy contain a lot of active verbs, or does it limp along with adjectives, adverbs, and other excessive parts of speech cluttering up its movement?

❑ Are the benefits of the product or service delineated in clear, concise fashion?

❑ Do the benefits of the product or service follow in logical sequence?

❑ Does the headline emphasize the main benefits of the product?

❑ Does every line of copy in some way reflect or state a benefit for the consumer?

❑ Are the benefits properly recapped in the copy at the end?

❑ If there is a coupon, is it clear and concise? Is there enough room to write in a name and address?

❑ Can the reader fill out the coupon easily and clip it for mailing without ruining the ad?

❑ Is the coupon composed and designed correctly for its particular purpose?

10

Keeping the Books

The only practical reason to start up a business is to make money. All other considerations are frosting on the cake. But you have always worked for someone else, and have been paid regular wages or a salary; you probably don't know much about keeping financial records.

All you need to know if you work for someone else is how much they pay you, and how much of your income is withheld by the federal government for income taxes and social security. What really matters to you is your regular pay check and how it is going to pay your household expenses.

In a normal household situation, you don't really need to keep books in order to handle your regular bills—electricity, fuel oil or gas, telephone, and so on. Bills are sent out; you pay them regularly. You keep your checkbooks in order so that you can figure out your income tax at the end of the year. The details are minimal.

Keeping Records of Cash Flow

However, once you start a business of your own, you must pay strict attention to the exact amount of money you earn and to the exact amount of money you use to pay your bills. If you fail to do so, you can easily lose money rather than make it. In order to pay strict attention to the inflow and outgo of money, you must keep accurate, detailed records of every penny you earn and spend.

There are two basic functions you have to understand in every business venture:

❏ One is to keep an accurate account of your financial standing so you can tell whether you are losing money or making money.

❏ The other is to bill your customers systematically in order to keep money owed you flowing in.

If you do not pay careful attention to these two basic functions, it is pointless for you to be in business in the first place.

The Business of Bookkeeping

One of the main chores in any business is bookkeeping. It is in the "books" that the record of your income and your expenditures are kept. You must be aware on a day-to-day basis of exactly how much money you make and how much money you spend. This is necessary not only for your own peace of mind, but for the government as well in the collection of business taxes.

In the main, you should be familiar with the two basic

types of bookkeeping. One is called single-entry book-keeping, the other double-entry bookkeeping.

For a very small business—a one-man operation, or a typical mom-and-pop proprietorship that is not too complicated—a single-entry type of bookkeeping can accurately keep track of a business operation.

Money In and Money Out—Single-Entry Bookkeeping

Single-entry bookkeeping simply records the movement of money in and out of your business. For example, for each day of the year you put down the total income you have received on that day and the total amount of money you have paid out to keep the business running.

Note that these sums have absolutely nothing to do with *personal* expenses. They pertain only to what you spend in the operation of the business. The trouble with some entrepreneurs who start out a business on their own is a blending of personal and business expenses—a mixture that tends to blur the real picture of the business's success or imminent failure.

The key to single-entry bookkeeping is the specific manner in which the income and the outgo of money is broken down into periods of time. In this way you can always check back to find out when you got that check for $50 for installing a backdoor lock. You can also find out exactly when you paid for the paint you used on another job.

At the end of each monthly period you then total all the income you made and enter that amount as *income* for the month. Then you add up all the money you paid out for bills that have to do with the business, and enter that as *expenditures,* or *expenses.*

A quick glance at the books will show you exactly how much money you brought in and how much money you took out of the business to pay for expenses.

The third part of the breakdown is called the *balance.*

You arrive at the *balance* by subtracting *expenditures* from *income*.

Income, Outgo, and Balance

To recap, in single-entry bookkeeping you break up your flow of cash into income and outgo, known as *income* and *expenditures*. In turn, each item is recorded on the day of the month it occurs. Days in which there is no income or outgo are simply skipped. Most days will have only one amount of income or outgo. If two checks come in during a one-day period, put each on a separate line. The same is true of outgo. If you spend money for two different items in one day, you should note each with the amount spent.

When you finish with one month, and subtract outgo from income, you will find that the balance has nothing really to do with your *true* profit. In fact, you may find yourself with a deficit balance—that is, a minus quantity— for the month. On the other hand, you may find yourself with a great deal more than your true monthly profit.

Setting Up a Single-Entry System

There is no rigid set of rules for inaugurating a single-entry bookkeeping system. Usually a sheet of blank paper is enough for a beginning. You don't need special ledger paper or other fancy types of bookkeeping equipment. It is, truly, a "come-as-you-are" kind of operation.

Five points are essential:

❑ day of month

❑ description of payment or expense

❑ total amount in

❑ total amount out

❑ balance

To begin with, divide the sheet of paper into five separate columns by running vertical lines all the way from the top of the paper to the bottom. Then label the first column, which should be a narrow one, *date*. The second column, which should be wide enough to write several words, *description*. The third column, which should be narrow and to the right of the page, is *total in*. The fourth column, narrow and to the right, *total out*. And the fifth column, at the right-hand edge of the sheet, is *balance*.

Date

The column under the word *date* is the date of the actual payment for a job or service, or the date of the actual payment of an expense.

Description

The wide column under the word *description* should be roomy enough to include a brief description of the job performed or of the item for which money is paid out.

Total In

The narrow column under *total in* represents the amount of money paid you for a job or item sold. If there is more than one payment on a single day list each separately and describe it accurately.

Total Out

The narrow column under *total out* represents any money you spend for supplies or other types of expenses. If there are more than one, list each item separately, with an adequate description.

Balance

The narrow column at the edge of the sheet under *balance* will show you exactly where you stand at the end of each day during the month—at least, cashwise. In some cases, depending on the cash flow, you will find that the sum represented is a minus quantity.

Here's an example of a typical informal single-entry bookkeeping system:

DATE	DESCRIPTION	TOTAL IN	TOTAL OUT	BALANCE
7/3	Roof repair Johnson house (6/14)	$175		$175
7/6	New ladder Smithers yard		$ 67	$108
7/6	3 gallons white paint, Hoffman job		$ 64	$ 44
7/8	3 strips aluminum flashing, Hoffman job		$ 15	$ 29
7/9	Garage window Watts house (6/12)	$ 98		$127
7/10	Repair work light		$ 18	$109
7/11	Lumber for Spence job		$110	$ − 1
7/11	Cleanup Royarson yard (6/30)	$250		$249
7/15	Painting Hoffman house (7/6)	$325		$574
7/20	Bricks and mortar, for Hoffman chimney		$137	$437
7/25	Work truck overhaul		$167	$270
7/28	Chimney repair, for Kissick house	$125		$395
JULY	INCOME:	$973		
JULY	EXPENSES:		$578	
JULY	BALANCE:			$395

Single-entry bookkeeping can give you an excellent picture of your work through the month. It does not, however, give you an accurate picture of your own total assets or your own position in relation to personal bills you owe.

More about that later.

Disadvantages to Single-Entry Bookkeeping

If you can confine your business—that is, if it is small enough and of a certain type—you can get along with single-entry bookkeeping. However, there are several disadvantages to this limited type of bookkeeping. Although you are able to see at a glance your income and your expenditures, you do not keep an adequate record of your total assets or liabilities. In addition, there is no built-in check for arithmetical accuracy.

But there is still another important difference between single-entry and double-entry bookkeeping. It has to do with the way in which you account for your income and outgo, that is, whether you choose to keep your books on a "cash" basis or on an "accrual" basis.

The Cash Basis

Note in the single-entry system shown above the first line, dated July 3: "Roof repair Johnson house (6/14)." The handyman keeping the records obviously performed the repair job in June, but was not paid until July 3. Note also line 5, for July 9: "Garage window Watts house (6/12)." Once again, the handyman is recording the fact that he received payment some days after doing the job.

This method of accounting is called the "cash" method. You record income *when you receive the cash,* and you record expenditures *when you pay for them.* (Incidentally, even if you are paid for your work by check, in accountant's terminology you deal in "cash.") The point is that unpaid bills due you and purchases do not show on the cash ledger, and this can give you a misleading picture of your income and outgo.

The Accrual Basis

"Accrual" accounting is the answer to this particular problem. You record all your income and expenses whether paid or not. All transactions are recorded when they are made, whether actual cash changes hands or not. In addition, every transaction has two separate entries—a "debit" and a "credit"—and not just one as in single-entry bookkeeping. Total debits equal total credits for the books to balance.

A simple bookkeeping system like the single-entry one presented above would work well for the services of a typical handyman. But if you sell anything, or if you are in a service business that stocks and sells parts, you must use the more complicated accrual method of bookkeeping to conform to federal tax law.

Of the three main types of business—service, product manufacture, and retail sales—only the first and perhaps a certain kind of the second can be handled on a cash basis.

Let's take a look at a typical double-entry system for a moment.

Setting Up a Double-Entry Bookkeeping System

Double-entry bookkeeping is a refinement of single-entry bookkeeping, involving some of the details discussed above.

In the handyman's records above, both income and outgo are recorded on the same sheet of paper, day in and day out.

The double-entry system involves *two* books (really,

177

sheets) rather than just one. One records income, the other records expenditures or outgo.

The Income Ledger

The income ledger is a double-entry system—actually a day-by-day record of all payments, sales, or money received. A typical income ledger contains thirty-one lines, with a number of columns across it, ending up with the total sales for each day, and a final total for the month at the bottom.

For the handyman above, no such income statement would be needed. But for the owner of a small shop, or even the owner of an active garage repair service, it would be necessary to keep a daily double-entry ledger.

The income ledger usually includes columns with *date, sales period, sales,* and *total sales.* Because of state and local taxes, many income ledgers break up *sales* into *taxable sales* and *sales tax* columns, with separate columns for *non-taxable sales,* and other miscellaneous headings.

Breakdown of Total Sales

The purpose of the income ledger is to record the *total* sales for each day of the month. It can show you at a glance exactly how much sales tax is owed for a particular day, and it can also show the interested state officials the details when they come around to check up on the ledger.

If you are involved in a business which has a moderate sales volume, you should keep your ledger up-to-date throughout the week. To do so, you add up all your sales slips for the day and enter the totals in the columns provided in the income ledger. By adding up the totals from left to right—taxable sales, sales tax, and non-taxable sales, you will get the same total as that in the right-hand column. (This is a good way to double-check your sales figures each day, incidentally.)

At the end of the month, add up the total for all monthly income. Be sure to do your final check for the month *during* the month and not over into the next month. Also be sure to add your totals for sales, sales tax, and non-taxable sales together at the bottom of the page to check against the grand total for the month in the last column. Check back to locate any errors.

At the end of the year, add up all twelve monthly totals on a year-end summary page usually provided in any income ledger book. Cross-check all totals of the interior columns with the total in the last column to detect errors.

The Credit Ledger

If your store is a small one you may not have any credit accounts. However, as you grow, you may set up a system of accounts for charge. For a credit account, you enter a credit sale in your income ledger in exactly the same way you enter a cash sale. However, in order not to lose track of the amount owed you, you must keep a separate ledger with all credit accounts listed and with the proper update.

For a simple operation, you can use what is called a credit ledger. This must be kept in addition to your income ledger. Each sale that is a credit sale must be entered not only in the income ledger with its amount but in the credit ledger as well.

A typical credit ledger has five columns: one for the *date* of the sale; another identifies the customer by *name;* another lists the items sold by *invoice number;* another lists the amount of the *sale,* including *sales tax* if any; and the last column is left to be filled in when the item is finally *paid* for.

How to Use the Credit Ledger

Each item must be listed separately in the credit ledger in order to keep the records straight. Use the credit sales slip at the time you make the sale or at the end of the day when you add up the total for your income ledger. Write *credit sale* on the receipt and file it in a separate place for quick reference.

When a bill is paid, write down the date in the *date paid* column. The advantage of the credit ledger is that you always have a handy reference to check on the number of items not yet paid for, along with the names of the customers who owe you money.

Some credit ledgers have an extra column for *remarks*. You can write down any past-due letters or other notices sent to try to collect delinquent payment. At the year's end if you feel that the bill is uncollectible—that is, if the customer has moved out of town or is otherwise obviously going to be unable to pay—mark the account *uncollectible* and file it in your *bad debts* folder. These can be considered an expense against your business when computed at the year's end.

The Expenditure Ledger

The expenditure ledger is the other side of the coin to the income ledger. In the expenditure book you record all your expenses against the business, including loan repayments, personal withdrawals against the company, and other expenses used to run the business. However, the most important function of the expenditure ledger is to classify different types of expenses for you. For that reason, there are separate columns in the typical ledger for such categories as office supplies, raw materials, postage, rent, utilities, and so on.

Of course there are hundreds of types of expenditures a company may have. The purpose of the expenditure ledger is to lump various individual expenditures into categories for quick and easy reference. What columns you use and what specific items you include in each category depends primarily on the kind of business you are running.

You can use certain columns to separate categories of expenditures because they may be important to you in preparing your income tax return. Other categories may be those sums you pay in large dollar amounts.

Different Designs of Ledgers

There are various models of expenditure ledgers, developed for small business of all kinds. Study them well before settling on one; your business will function better if you use the proper one.

The best time to fill in sums in the expenditure ledger is the moment you make the payment. As soon as you pay anything in cash, write down the amount and the pertinent data immediately. It is amazing how quickly you can forget a transaction in cash, or remember the amount inaccurately.

If you pay a bill by check, record the information in your checkbook: check number, date, amount, payee, and a description of what the payment is for. Then copy the information into the expenditure ledger.

There are, in fact, expenditure ledgers that are combined with checkbooks for your convenience. It all depends on what makes you more comfortable to work with.

Making Use of the Expenditure Ledger

Use the expenditure ledger the same way you use your income ledger. Total all the columns of the expenditure ledger each month. Cross-check the totals with the grand total column, and work back to correct any mistakes.

Do not, however, start a new expenditure ledger each month. If a month ends in the middle of the page, simply draw a double line across, skip two lines, and start the next month right there.

At the end of the year add up the monthly totals of the columns and enter them on the summary sheet at the end of the ledger. Now comes the so-called accrual procedure. Remember that under this system of accounting, all expenses are recorded whether they are paid out or not. For one reason or another, you may not have paid one or more of your bills.

It is at the end of the year that you must make out a list of all bills you have not yet paid. As you enter each unpaid bill, mark it *accounts payable.* You must also add any other unpaid expenses for the year—taxes or the like—putting each on a separate line, even if you have never received a bill for any of them.

Final Check for Expenditures

Total all the columns and cross-check your totals to see that everything adds up both vertically and horizontally. This is your final check for expenditures. If there are errors, work back and correct them.

Now total any returned checks and uncollectible accounts in your bad debts folder, and enter these sums in the grand total column.

The unpaid bills and expenses that have not been billed at the end of the year are deductible the year they were incurred—the year just ended. You may not deduct them again the following year, even though they may be paid then. When the bills are paid you will note that they are marked *accounts payable* and they must be entered in the non-deductible column for the coming year.

You can easily design your own income and expenditure ledgers, working out the most convenient and efficient method for handling your finances.

Assets, Liabilities, and Net Worth

Now about the big three:

❑ assets

❑ liabilities

❑ net worth

The income ledger and the expenditure ledger are closed out at the end of the fiscal year. Your fiscal year may run from January 1 through December 31. Or, if you choose, your fiscal year may run from any day you choose through 365 days. Your particular business may dictate selecting a fiscal year that runs quite different from the calendar year.

It is at the end of the fiscal year that both income and expenditure ledgers will be totaled and closed. Some double-entry systems also record assets, liabilities, and net worth.

These three ledgers do not end with each fiscal year, but continue year after year, without break. The idea of these three books is for you to be able to check back and examine your total worth through the months and years.

The "Self-Balancing" Method

The rationale for these other record systems is obvious. Your daily income and outgo really have very little to do with your own net worth. Daily expenses and earnings come and go, more or less unevenly. However, your liabilities remain for a much longer period of time. For example, rent, insurance, and equipment bought on time will continue as expenses for a long time until they are finally paid off.

Any double-entry record is called "self-balancing." That means that every list of debits and credits must total out, total debits equaling total credits. When these columns are shifted over into the ledger accounts, the debits will equal the credits; the accounts are "in balance."

Of course, on a day-to-day basis, debits do not equal credits. Accounts receivable and accounts payable always upset any such "balance." Certain amounts like that must be carried over from one month to the next, or from one year to the next.

How the Business Is Going

It is common practice to make out a financial statement at the end of each month, then enter these figures into the ledgers. In the long run, the income statement shows how the operation of the business is proceeding through the year.

The payouts are also an indication of the same thing. In addition, the balance sheet shows you exactly where you stand at the end of a certain period in terms of total assets, liabilities, and net worth.

For a person running a complex operation like a small store, or a larger business employing a half dozen people, the double-entry system is essential.

Personal Expenses vs. Business Expenses

Assuming for the moment that your business is not overly large and is a fledgling enterprise, you can survive by using single-entry bookkeeping. However, there is more to keeping track of records than simple financial entries. You must always consider the money itself—and where it is at a given instant.

For example, everyone—including an entrepreneur—must eat and clothe himself or herself. He or she must pay rent or pay off a mortgage on a house. The problem is, how do you keep track of your non-business expenses so that your business expenses won't be hopelessly confused?

You must keep your business assets in a separate bank account that is in no way connected with your personal or family account. When you are paid for a job you have done, it is a temptation to put the money directly into your personal checking account to pay for next week's meals. Don't do it.

It is simply bad business.

Keeping a Business Diary or Record

The same is true of paying personal bills such as clothing accounts or college expenses. These bills must be paid out of your personal account, and not out of your business account. The two must be kept separate, or the muddle that ensues will be enough to put you out of business.

In addition, it can be a temptation to withdraw money from your business account to pay a bill in cash. However, it is better for you to pay the bill by check—on your business checking account—rather than by withdrawing the money. You will have a permanent record on your books and also in your canceled checks.

For penny ante expenditures—highway tolls, copying expenses—keep a diary. You can establish a petty cash fund for these.

The Use of Receipts

Sometimes it happens that you might want to pay an expense with cash. If you do, write out a check to yourself and present it at the bank to get the cash. Get a receipt for this cash payment and write down a statement of it in your records to explain where the money went.

You should support all your entries in your books with

185

canceled checks, paid bills, duplicate deposit slips, or any other items that document your expenses. These must be filed and stored. The IRS may want to see them.

If you have to move money from your business account to your personal account to pay a personal bill, make sure that the transaction is described as such in your business records so that it will not throw the figures off. As soon as you can, you should put the money back into your business account.

Setting Up an Accounts Receivable System

Aside from the implementation of a satisfactory book-keeping system to keep you constantly aware of the inflow and outflow of money, make sure you are receiving payment for all outstanding debts—a crucial function of any business operation.

The term *accounts receivable* refers to all bills that have been issued but not paid by purchasers. Because a great many small businesses now use credit as a basis for payment, it is incumbent upon the proprietor to keep a constant eye on the amounts of money owed.

In times of tight money, people in all walks of life tend to take a leisurely and laid-back attitude toward the payment of bills. Runaway nonpayment of bills is a sure indication of imminent insolvency in a business. To put it another way, being in business is tantamount to being in the business of collecting money owed.

The credit ledger, as described above, is one of the simplest types of accounts receivable systems, but it is by no means the only way to keep yourself up-to-date on money owed. There are at least two other systems you can initiate if a credit ledger becomes outgrown or for any reason proves ineffective. Here are the two of them:

❏ card-tickler system

❏ duplicate invoice system

The Card-Tickler System

Instead of a credit ledger, you can always employ a separate file that will keep you apprised of accounts receivable. This is an especially good system if you have a large number of customers or clients.

The base of the system is a special file in which you insert a card for every bill that is not paid. On the card you write down the amount of the bill, the terms, the date due, and of course the name of the person or company who owes you the money.

To make the file work, you divide the compartment into thirty-one sections, one for each day of the month. You then put each card in the proper slot to take care of it as the date comes up on the calendar. Taking care of it means simply opening up File Number 5 on May 5, for example, and checking through the list of delinquents.

The Duplicate Invoice System

This file resembles the card-tickler system, but works in reverse. You make an extra copy of any bill or invoice and keep it in a file. You arrange your duplicate invoices in a file of thirty-one separate sections, exactly as the card-tickler system provides.

When you receive money for payment, you destroy the extra copy so that it will not appear again. Each day you check through the invoices for bills that are not paid. The bills left over become the list of accounts receivable, similar to the cards in the card-tickler system.

How to Collect Overdue Bills

Just because someone owes you money does not necessarily mean you are going to get it by reminding them.

Collecting overdue bills has become a major headache for all types of businesses, particularly in years of high inflation and tight budgets.

Usually the best way to proceed in dunning for money is to create a series of letters to your debtors: the first, a mild reminder that money is owed; the second, a little stronger reminder; the third, an assertive reminder; the fourth, even stronger; and so on. If you have set up a reasonably effective system of accounts receivable, you will be able to send out these letters of past-due accounts as your tickler file or credit ledger shows you who is delinquent.

A Time Schedule for Past-Due Letters

Generally speaking, you should allow a creditor at least thirty days for the normal payment of a bill—that is, thirty days after the original bill has been sent out if the billing method is monthly; or thirty days after the purchase of the item in the store if you are working on a charge account system.

At the end of thirty days, it is up to you to remind your customer that he or she owes you money. This statement should be no more than a simple reminder. It should be nothing more than a notation of the amount owed and when the debt was incurred.

At the end of forty-five days, you should send out a *reminder* of the bill, pointing out that it is now *overdue*. The message should be that the bill has become delinquent, but that if the debtor pays up, he or she won't be charged interest or other penalties.

At the end of sixty days, the third communication should go out. This is a message worded in firm tones. It should specify one point:

Pay now!

If you are supplying products for a manufacturer, you should point out that all shipments will be held up until the bill is paid. For a customer of a store, this should be the first message of urgency.

At the end of seventy-five days, the fourth communication goes out. This message is more than urgent; it is tantamount to a threat. If the debtor doesn't pay up, you will turn the account over to a collection agency. This should not be an idle threat, either. If you find yourself with many bills seventy-five days overdue, it is a clear danger to your company's solvency.

At the end of ninety days—three months—a fifth letter should go out. This is the letter that informs the debtor that you are taking action, either by a collection agency, a case in the small claims court, or an attorney. The time this action is to go into effect should be stated, leaving a loophole for the debtor to pay up.

The Four Stages of Collections

The preparation of the letters asking the debtor to pay up must be done in such a way that the customer is not turned off entirely—in the event, for example, that there is an honest and unavoidable holdup of money. At the same time, the tone of the letters should be firm and unrelenting.

There are four stages of intensity to these letters:

- ❑ the gentle hint
- ❑ the straight appeal
- ❑ the hard push
- ❑ the big shove

The hint stage includes notification of the debt, and the reminder of the debt. In the hinting stage, you pretend that the debtor has simply forgotten about the debt, or is unaware of it. Your rationale for the letter is to *remind*—not to dun.

189

Once this stage is over, you move into the appeal stage, in which you begin to work on the psychology of the debtor. The appeal may come from many different angles, but every single one of these has an emotional thrust. This stage is complex and may involve any number of different types of appeal.

After reminders and appeals have been proved to be ineffective, you move on to the hard-push stage. This usually takes place on about the ninetieth day past due, as has been explained earlier. This is the stage in which you make threats to take the account to a collection agency, or to small claims court.

If the hard-push stage doesn't work either, then you move into the final stage—the big-shove stage. This involves collection of the debt by legal effort. There are several ways you can do this. You can go to a small claims court and sue the debtor. You can put your overdue account in the hands of a professional collection agency. Or you can turn the account over to a lawyer.

Computerizing the Office Bookkeeping

Since bookkeeping is basically a matter of filing and retrieving information—that is, in writing down figures for future reference—you can do it in a number of ways. You can use books and ledgers as has been explained. Or you can make use of computers. With a floppy disk you can keep your own books and even set up a system of accounts receivable, including the mailing of letters of reminder and appeal.

The personal computer has revolutionized the operation of the small-business office, and opened the way to a less expensive office operation for the individual proprietor. For the larger business, there are larger computers that deal in much more sophisticated systems.

The personal computer can perform three basic functions in the role of data processing:

190

❏ the filing of information (storage and retrieval)
❏ the computation of arithmetic (addition, subtraction, multiplication, and division)
❏ the comparison of values

It can also:

❏ store data
❏ classify data
❏ sort names
❏ sort numbers
❏ calculate
❏ summarize

Computer literature is a burgeoning segment of the publications industry. You can find out a great deal of detailed information about personal computers and the software programs that make them work by looking through the available publications.

Pleasing the IRS

Federal taxes payable to the Internal Revenue Service are determined strictly according to the type of business organization involved. Each type of business pays on a different basis. For every type of business there is a specific form to be filled out. The three types of business organization are:

- ❑ sole proprietorship
- ❑ partnership
- ❑ corporation

For the sole proprietorship and the partnership, the IRS does not exact taxes directly from the business itself, but rather from the proprietor or the individual partner. That is, the proprietor or partner includes the profits or losses made in the business on his or her personal income tax return.

For the corporation, the situation is different. Except for the S corporation, the profits of any corporation are taxed both to the corporation and to the shareholders when the profits are distributed. To put it in another way, the corporation itself is taxed for its profits to begin with; a separate form is used for this. Then each member is taxed as an individual on his or her personal income tax form.

Let's take up these three important different divisions one by one.

Taxing the Sole Proprietor

In a sole proprietorship, your business has no specific existence apart from you as the owner. Your company's liabilities are your own personal liabilities, and your proprietary interest ends at your death.

When you figure your taxable income for the year, you add in any profit, and subtract any loss, from your sole proprietorship. To report this on your yearly income tax, you use Schedule C (Form 1040). The amount of profit or loss on Schedule C is then entered as an item of profit or loss on Form 1040.

In addition, if you are a sole proprietor and do not work for someone else who is paying half of your social security benefits, you are liable for what is called a self-employment tax. Usually, you will be required to file estimated tax payment forms four times a year—along with a check for the estimated payment.

Taxing the Partnership

Like the sole proprietorship, the partnership is not taxed as a partnership separately. Nevertheless, the partnership is required to figure its profit or loss and file it on Form 1065. For tax purposes, the term "partnership" includes a partnership, a syndicate, a group, a pool, a joint venture, or other unincorporated ventures, including an unincorporated organization that is carrying on a business and that cannot be classified as a trust, estate, or corporation.

193

NOTE: A joint undertaking formed to share expenses is *not* a partnership. The co-ownership of property maintained and leased or rented does *not* necessarily constitute a partnership. If co-owners provide service to tenants, a partnership exists.

A partner's share of income, gain, loss, deductions, or credits, is usually determined by the original partnership agreement drawn up at the time the arrangement was established. Such an agreement may be modified for a particular tax year after the close of the year, but not later than the date for filing the partnership return.

Taxing the Corporation

The profits of a corporation are taxed originally against the corporate body. Then, when the profits are distributed to the members of the corporation, the dividends are taxed. In figuring taxable income, a corporation generally takes the same deductions as a sole proprietorship and is entitled to special deductions. A corporation is required to file Form 1120.

"Corporation" includes a joint stock company, an insurance company, or a trust and partnership that actually operates as an association or a corporation.

An S corporation (subchapter corporation) is taxed in a slightly different manner—that is, if it chooses. It may desire exemption from federal income tax. Then all of its shareholders include their share of the corporation's items of income, deduction, loss, and credit, or share the non-separately-computed income or loss in their individual income. It may have to pay a tax on excess net passive income or a tax on capital gains. An S corporation, as has been noted, must have no more than thirty-five shareholders.

Employer Identification Number (EIN)

A sole proprietor can use his or her social security number in reporting profits or losses. However, a partnership, corporation, trust, or estate must have an employer identification number (EIN) to use as its taxpayer identification number.

NOTE: A sole proprietor—if he or she pays wages to one or more employees, or is required to file excise tax returns, including those for alcohol, tobacco, or firearms—must also have an EIN.

Figuring Profit and Loss

Although the computations at times may be fairly complex, the actual determination of profit and loss is simple in outline. To compute profit is simply to establish the difference between *gross income* and *business deductions*.

❏ *Gross income* is all the money that comes in to you before you make any deductions for business. It is the total amount of sales, fees, and commissions.

❏ *Net income* is determined by subtracting all your *business deductions* and *expenses* from your *gross income*.

What a Business Deduction Is

A business deduction is an expense related to the running of an enterprise. Some business expenses are not deductible in the computation of your income tax, however. To be a legitimate business expense that can be deducted, it must meet the IRS's rule of four:

195

(1) The expense must be incurred in connection with your business. It cannot be a personal, or nonbusiness expense.

(2) The expense must be ordinary and necessary—that is, it must be commonly accepted to be a business expense in your particular type of business; or it must be an expense that is appropriate in developing and maintaining your business.

(3) The expense must be for items used reasonably fast. That is, the expense cannot be counted for equipment that is used for more than a year—machinery, tools, furniture. For these items, you have to prorate the expense over the useful life of the asset.

(4) The expense can be of any amount, as long as it is reasonable.

In many cases, especially in the case of a sole proprietor, the expense may concern something that is used not only for business but for personal use as well—a car, for example. In that case, you must allocate a certain portion of the use of the car to your business and certain portion to your personal use. This allocation can be complicated and will be explained later.

If you have purchased an item in the past but have not used it for your business, you can begin depreciating it during the year you begin to use it for business purposes. It doesn't matter when you bought the item.

Figuring Business Expenses

It is in the computation of business expenses that you can run afoul of the IRS. Even if you choose only the proper and legitimate deduction, you may figure it incorrectly or slip up in one way or another. For the most part, the items on Schedule C are self-explanatory—but in some instances you should know exactly how the IRS views the deduction.

Here are some that might be considered somewhat moot:

Bad Debts from Sales or Services

You can deduct business bad debts—rubber checks and other uncollectible accounts—but you should keep records to document these for the IRS if it asks. There is one exception: if you use the cash method of accounting, you cannot take a bad debt expense for unpaid and uncollectible accounts. The reason for this is obvious: you did not record the amount as income in the first place. However, you can count bounced checks because they were posted in the income ledger and you do have a record of them.

Car and Truck Expenses

This section can cause a great deal of pain and grief unless it is perfectly understood. You can take all expenses in operating a vehicle for business purposes as a deduction if you exclude commuting expenses between your home and your place of work (this is a personal expense, according to the way the IRS looks at it).

There are two ways in which to figure car expenses. One is the yearly car expense, and the other is allocating car expenses to a yearly mileage rate.

(1) Yearly Car Expense

Let's suppose you are using your car for a business you run as an individual proprietor. During the year you estimate that you use the car about 60 percent of the time for your business, and about 40 percent of the time for your own personal use. Obviously you can deduct only that portion of the car's expenses that has to do with the business—the 60 percent amount.

197

You must keep itemized records of all car expenses, including gasoline, oil, lubrication, maintenance, repairs, insurance, parking and tolls, garage rents, license and registration fees, and auto club dues.

You can even depreciate the amount of the car's purchase price over its "useful" life. In addition, you are required to depreciate certain major items that will last over one year such as batteries, tires, or an engine overhaul.

Keeping itemized records of all these expenses is a great deal of trouble. In addition, the complex calculations used in depreciating batteries, tires, and so on make for a lot of extra headaches. And so the IRS has come up with an alternate plan, the standard mileage rate.

(2) Standard Mileage Rate

Instead of keeping records of every oil change, every lube job, every maintenance chore, and so on, you simply figure out how much use you make of your car in your business and then find out how many miles you have driven your car for business purposes during the year. Say you drove the car 15,000 miles, and used your car for business about 11,000. Your mileage for the year—for business purposes—would be 11,000.

The IRS each year allows you a certain figure per mile traveled. For 1983 it was 20.5 cents a mile. You then multiply your business miles by 20.5 to find out how much you are allowed to deduct. It would be $2,255 for the above situation (11,000 × 20.5 = $2,255).

If you travel over 15,000 miles for your business, you cannot take the full amount (20.5 cents) but must use the amount set by the IRS (11 cents for each mile over 15,000 in 1983).

There are restrictions. You must own your car, not use it for hire as a taxi, not operate a fleet of cars using two or more, not have claimed depreciation using any other method than straight line, not have claimed additional first-year depreciation on the car, and not have claimed a section 179 (expense) deduction on the car.

Whether you use the yearly car expense or the standard mileage rate method depends a lot on the kind of car you are using. A large gas-guzzler that requires expensive maintenance might prove to be more deductible under the yearly car expense method than the standard mileage rate, while a small economical car would prove more deductible using the standard mileage rate.

Freight

This item refers to shipping charges—in both directions. "Freight-in" means shipping to you. "Freight-out" means shipping out the goods you sell. Don't forget to include "freight-in" charges on merchandise and materials you are carrying in inventory and purchased for resale. It must be included as part of the cost.

Freight-in on depreciable fixed assets like equipment and furniture must be added to the cost of the asset and depreciated. Freight-out and shipping charges on goods sold are fully deductible.

Insurance

You can deduct all current business-related insurance premiums you pay. These include fire, extended coverage, liability, theft, business interruption, automobile, workmen's compensation, group insurance premiums, unemployment, surety, and fidelity bonds. Note that you must not include automobile insurance under "cars and trucks" if you include it under insurance.

Personal health insurance premiums and life insurance premiums are not deductible as a business expense.

If you happen to pay insurance premiums covering more than a year, you are allowed to deduct only the current year's portion. Even if you use the cash method of accounting and actually pay the cash in a specified year, the IRS will not allow a deduction for prepaid insurance extending beyond that one year.

Repairs

Figuring out the amount of deduction you can claim on repairs you make to your property used in trade or business is a bit complicated. From a tax standpoint, any repair falls into one of two categories:

❑ It is a deductible expense.

❑ It is a capital expenditure.

A capital expenditure is not deductible. What you spend to keep your property in a normal and efficient operating condition is deductible as an expense. But what you spend on adding to the value of your property or significantly increasing its life is not deductible as an expense, because it is a capital gain. Capital expenditures can be deducted through depreciation deductions.

In order to understand the difference between a repair and an improvement, let's take a look at some specifics.

Repairs

If you patch up and repair a floor, you are making a legitimate business repair. If you repaint the inside and outside of a building used in your business, you are making a deductible repair. If you fix roofs and gutters and mend leaks in the building where you work, you are making a legitimate deductible repair.

Note that a repair does not add to the value or usefulness of property, nor does it add to the life of the property. The cost of the repair, including labor, supplies, and certain other items, is a deductible expense. (Note: You cannot deduct the value of your own labor—only the labor of someone else.)

Improvement

If you put in new electric wiring, you are making an improvement in your property, increasing its value and its usage. If you put on a new roof, or a new floor, you are improving your property. If you install new plumbing, you are also improving it. If you strengthen weakened walls that might fall down, you are improving property, not "repairing" it in a tax sense.

Other Nondeductibles

You cannot deduct the cost of replacements, either. A replacement stops deterioration and adds to the life of your property. It must be capitalized and depreciated. However, if you replace parts of a machine that only keep it in normal operating condition, then you can treat the replacements as repairs and deduct the cost of them as a business expense.

Deductible and Nondeductible Expenses

The IRS lists the following examples of deductible and nondeductible expenses:

❑ Vehicles used in business. You capitalize the cost of a car or truck; therefore it is not deductible. Repairs to vehicles may be deducted.

❑ Roads and driveways. Building a road or driveway to your business property is a capital expenditure and cannot be deducted. Maintaining a private road, however, is deductible as a necessary business expense.

❑ Tools. Any tool that is worn out, thrown away, and replaced is a legitimate business expense and can be deducted.

❑ Machinery. The cost of replacing parts of a machine is deductible as an ordinary expense.

❑ Heating equipment. Changing from one type of heating system to another is a capital expenditure and cannot be deducted.

Travel and Entertainment

The Internal Revenue Service doesn't always look at travel in the same way you might. Even if you have to go to Paris to meet a few business contacts (and take your wife or husband along to spend a little time vacationing) you cannot deduct the entire trip as a business expense. Legitimate business travel expenses are deductible—but the rules are specific.

If the reason for the trip is mainly personal, you cannot deduct any of the travel expense. If it is mainly business, you can deduct the percentage of the whole that you allocated to business.

Travel that is all business is all deductible.

The above points relate to travel outside the United States. If you are on a business trip inside the United States, you can deduct the entire amount of the trip, even if some of the trip is for pleasure.

Travel expenses include:

- cost of transportation for yourself and luggage to and from destination
- meals and lodging
- cost of transportation away from home—taxi fares, auto rentals, and so forth
- business entertainment
- laundry, dry cleaning, barbering, and so on
- telephone
- tips and incidentals

Entertainment is something else again. This is an expense that the IRS will always look at closely. You must keep detailed records of all entertainment expenses and you must be prepared to justify them.

Basically, any entertainment expense directly related to

the conduct of a business is deductible. A meal is allowable. Be sure to get a receipt and note on it who you took to lunch and why. The cost of a party to promote your business is deductible. So is the food served at a business meeting, and the food provided to employees on the premises.

The important thing to do to justify entertainment expenses is to keep good records.

Office in the Home

If you are an entrepreneur of the new stripe, so to speak, it may well be that you choose to work not out of an office but out of your own home. If you do so, you are allowed to deduct a certain amount of money for expenses as "rent" for using your home in lieu of an office.

This can be a tricky business because of the limitations imposed upon the entrepreneur. Although working in the home may save the individual proprietor $6,000 a year in office rent, he or she cannot deduct that $6,000. The taxpayer must allocate the amount of expense in quite a different way.

Allocation of the Proper Percentage

For example, let's suppose that you work out of your own home during the first year of your new business venture. You have a six-room house. You use one room of the house strictly for business purposes. That is, the room is not a television or lounging room that you use only during working hours as an office. You use it all the time exclusively as an office—twenty-four hours a day, if need be.

In that case, you can allocate 16 percent—one sixth— of your household expenses—that is, the amount of money it takes to run the household (heat, light, rent, and so on)—to your business expenses. Let's say that it costs about $6,600 a year to run your house. You simply divide $6,600 by 6 (since you use one full room out of six rooms) to find your allocation for expenses in lieu of office space.

203

"Business Use of Your Home"

If you work part-time, or full-time for someone else, it's not a good idea to claim this expense—use of home in lieu of office space—because you will have to calculate the percentage of total working time you spend at home and calculate that percentage against the percentage of the household expenses. Forget it.

The IRS issues a brochure, publication 587, "Business Use of Your Home," if you want to check any of these facts out.

WARNING: The IRS takes a dim view of using the home in lieu of office, and even includes a line in the current forms that alert it to this practice. If you mark that line as you must if you take the office cost it's waving a red flag for the IRS to audit your records.

Incidentally, if you do take an expense like this, you simply write it down on Schedule C in one of the blank lines provided in the section on deductions.

A Little About Depreciation

Figuring depreciation can be a complicated pastime. Don't forget that you have to depreciate any capital expenditure rather than deduct it as an expense. The purpose of depreciation is to spread the cost of an asset over a number of years—"it's useful life," in the IRS phrase. Each year you can take off a portion of the cost as a deduction.

You must determine three things before you begin to compute depreciation:

(1) The basis of the depreciation.

(2) The date the item was placed in service.

(3) The method of depreciation.

Basis of the Depreciation

"Basis" refers to the amount of the property you own. For a piece of property that you buy, your original basis is the cost to you. If you inherit property, receive it as a gift, or build it yourself, you have to figure out your original basis in some other way. Improvement can increase basis; casualty losses can decrease basis.

Date the Item Was Placed in Service

For depreciation purposes, property is considered placed in service when it is in a condition or state of readiness and availability for an assigned function. Of course the assigned function must have direct bearing on the business you run.

Methods of Depreciation

There are several different types of depreciation methods:

❑ Accelerated Cost Recovery System (ACRS)

❑ Straight-line, declining balance, and sum of the year's digits methods

❑ Section 179 deduction

However, you must use ACRS for all tangible property placed in service after 1980, unless "specifically prevented." Intangible property is specifically prevented.

How ACRS Works

Under ACRS, all property is depreciated over three-year, five-year, ten-year, or fifteen-year recovery periods.

❑ Three-year property includes personal property with a

short, useful life such as cars, tractors, light-duty trucks, and special manufacturing tools.

❑ Five-year property includes office equipment, office furniture, and office fixtures.

❑ Ten-year property includes real property—public utility property—and manufactured homes, like mobile homes.

❑ Fifteen-year property includes all real property, such as buildings, other than that designated as ten-year property.

Each year you are allowed to take a certain percentage of the property in question. The table below shows how it works:

YEAR	3-YEAR CLASS	5-YEAR CLASS	10-YEAR CLASS
First year	25 percent	15 percent	8 percent
Second year	38 percent	22 percent	14 percent
Third year	37 percent	21 percent	12 percent
Fourth year		21 percent	10 percent
Fifth year		21 percent	10 percent
Sixth year			10 percent
Seventh year			9 percent
Eighth year			9 percent
Ninth year			9 percent
Tenth year			9 percent

Straight-Line, Declining Balance, and Sum of the Years Digits Method

Straight-line depreciation, and sum of the years digits depreciation are allowed only on property placed in service after December 31, 1980.

A Section 179 Deduction

The IRS allows you to treat the cost of certain qualifying properties as expenses rather than as capital expenditures. Naturally, as an expense, you can take off the entire amount of the cost the first year the properties are put into service.

You must make the decision at first whether you want to take the property as a direct expense, or to capitalize and depreciate the cost of the property.

There is a limit to the amount you can take for a Section 179 deduction: $5,000 for 1984.

If you file as a single person, you are allowed only one half the amount specified above. If you are a husband and wife filing separate returns, the "half" rule is applicable.

If you use property for both business and nonbusiness requirements, you are eligible to take a Section 179 deduction. You must allocate the cost of the property to reflect only the business use. Multiply the cost of the property by the percentage of business use. This is the adjusted cost that you are allowed to deduct.

Reporting Self-Employment Tax

The entrepreneur is required by the IRS to pay a tax for being in business for himself or herself. This is called the self-employment tax. Actually, it is a parallel tax to the social security tax, with the exception that the self-employed entrepreneur pays about twice the amount the hired worker pays.

If you are running a business on the side, and are employed by a firm that withholds your income tax and your

207

social security tax (called FICA), then you do not have to fill out Schedule SE, Form 1040 (self-employment tax). However, if you are on your own and make money during the year, you are liable to pay self-employment tax.

The amount you are required to pay is computed on Schedule SE. The amount is then added to the second page of Form 1040. Note that you not only pay income tax on page one—the amount that you make in your entrepreneurial efforts—but you pay it again on page two. That is, you pay income tax on a specific amount; and you pay self-employment tax on that amount in another line as well.

Like social security, self-employment tax has a maximum base amount each year. The amount appears on Schedule SE, along with the amount of the self-employment tax for the year. It keeps rising each year, just like social security.

For example, for the year 1984, the cap on self-employment and social security taxes was $37,800. If you made any more money than that, you paid a maximum of $4,271.40 if you were self-employed. But if you made $20,000, for example, you paid $2,260—an amount equal to the product of $20,000 and 11.3 percent ($20,000 × .113 = $2,260).

Afterword

The successful entrepreneur is not born, bred, or trained. He or she is not recognized until after proof of successful entrepreneurship has been demonstrated. The elements of character and personality that make up the successful business genius have been identified and studied.

Nevertheless, it is the individual composition of those particular diverse elements welded into an identifiable whole that makes a business go and creates a new star in the sky. Half the battle in building your own business is in developing your confidence that you can do the job. Decisiveness and determination can then be used as propellants to move the enterprise into action.

There are many different right ways to approach business situations. By making yourself aware of them, you have a much better chance of doing the right thing at the right time once you decide you want to control your own destiny in the business world.

By now you know all the character and personality

traits necessary to be a successful entrepreneur. You have at your fingertips the knowledge needed to move ahead by yourself.

The best of luck! It's out there waiting for you—

The Chance of a Lifetime

CHANCE OF A LIFETIME CONTEST

Official Rules

To enter, type your name and address on the top of a plain piece of paper, 8½" × 11". On the same piece of paper, describe your new business idea in 100 words or less and tell us why you think it would be a success. You must base your explanation on the theories and concepts found in the book, *Chance of a Lifetime* by Bill Adler.

Your entire answer must be legibly printed or typed. Mail your entry plus $1.00 processing fee payable to VENTURA ASSOCIATES, INC. (cash, check, or money order) to: CHANCE OF A LIFETIME CONTEST, P.O. Box 511, Lowell, IN 46399. Enter as often as you wish, but each entry must be mailed separately and must be accompanied by the $1.00 processing fee. All entries must be received by June 2, 1986. All entries become the property of Warner Books, Inc.

Entries will be reviewed by VENTURA ASSOCIATES, INC., an independent judging organization whose decision is final. Entries will be judged on the following criteria: application of themes in the book *Chance of a Lifetime* by Bill Adler (25%), creativity (20%), filling a need in the marketplace (20%), practicality (20%), and clarity of explanation (15%). In case of a tie, a tie-breaking question will be provided.

The grand prize winner will be awarded $25,000. This prize is guaranteed to be awarded.

Contest open to residents of the United States, 18 years of age or older. Employees and their families of Warner Books, Inc., Bill Adler Books, Inc., their respective affiliates and advertising agencies and VENTURA ASSOCIATES, INC., are not eligible. This contest is void where prohibited. All federal, state, and local laws and regulations apply.

No substitution for the prize. The prize is not transferable. Taxes are the responsibility of the winner. The winner agrees to sign an affidavit of eligibility. The winner's name and likeness may be used for publicity purposes.

For the name of the contest winner, send a stamped, self-addressed envelope to: CHANCE OF A LIFETIME WINNER, P.O. Box 666, Lowell, IN 46399.

A FINAL WORD

Soon somebody will have my check for $25,000. I have my fingers crossed that you will be that person but since (although we haven't met) I am confident you are not a greedy person—why don't you tell a friend or relative about this book—someone you really care about who has that dream of going into their own business.

Sure, I would like to sell some more books but that is not my main motivation—I want as many people as possible to have that chance of a lifetime.

I know that we are going to hear from you but we would also like to hear from some people you know and give them a chance of a lifetime, too.

Good luck! I just can't wait to put my check for $25,000 into somebody else's hands so they can be on their way toward financial independence with their own business.

Bill Adler